A Wave-Particle Theory of Conscious Awareness

(A Philosophical Viewpoint)

Mind, Machine & Morality
Is Experience a Quantum Field?

(2025 updated edition)

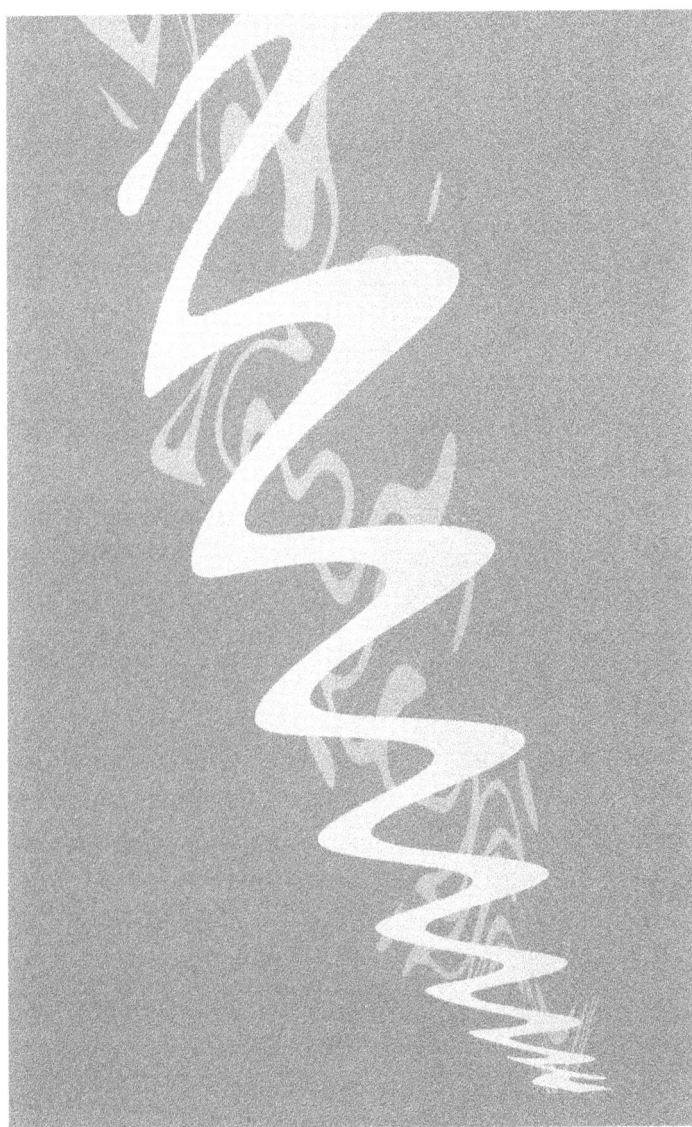

A Wave-Particle Theory of Conscious Awareness

(A Philosophical Viewpoint)

Mind, Machine & Morality
Is Experience a Quantum Field?

(2025 updated edition)

CARTER BLAKELAW
JACK CALVERLEY

The Logic of Dreams

The Solipsist

I called for help, but no one came,
I cried for love, that too in vain,
I sought the food to feed my mind,
But only found an unkind mess of fools.

- Carter Blakelaw, 2022

Also from The Logic of Dreams:

Fiction

GLUE, Elhamat & other stories... (SF Short Stories)
Science fiction, author Jack Calverley

Death of a Bad Neighbour (Revenge is Criminal)
Crime anthology, editor Jack Calverley

TINNITUS
Crime novel, author Jack Calverley

Nonfiction

The Man in My Head Has Lost His Mind
What makes us conscious? Author Carter Blakelaw

This Robot Brain Gets Life
Designing an AI that is all but conscious, author Carter Blakelaw

Authentic Art in the Age of AI
What we can do that an AI cannot, author Carter Blakelaw

CB's Top 100 Writing Tips, Tricks, Techniques and Tools...
100 rules of thumb for writing fiction, author Carter Blakelaw

Free updates on Patreon:

https://patreon.com/JackCalverley

Contents

Introduction

IN RIDLEY SCOTT'S 1982 movie *Blade Runner*, Rick Deckard asks Eldon Tyrell, the head of the corporation that created Rachael: "How can it not know what it is?"

Rachael is a *replicant* and *replicants* are almost indistinguishable from humans. Exceptionally, Rachael has been gifted false memories so she believes she is human and believes she has lived a normal human life up to that moment in the story.

However, whether or not she believes she's human, would 'I am human' be an adequate answer to the question: "Do you know what you are?"

We are human, but how illuminating is it to say: 'I am human'?

I have such-and-such number of chromosomes; I originate from planet Earth; my species has included Aristotle, Shakespeare, and Einstein. As to what *I-me-myself* am, well...

There is plenty more to describe and yet do we ever get to the core? In a very real sense we humans cannot ourselves claim to know what we are.

We *might* say we are conscious thinking beings who breathe air, eat food, have four limbs, walk upright, and so on. But this is description, not explanation. It does not reveal the essence.

Besides, what is a conscious, thinking being?

How is that trick pulled?

You only have to dig a little to discover we do not know what we are.

We are forced to talk in terms of neurons and brain chemistry, psychological tendencies, human languages, social behaviour, culture and so on. But any such talk merely scratches the surface of what consciousness might be, what thinking is, and what we are; it is description not explanation.

We do not know what we are.

How can we be so ignorant?

The answer is that such knowledge is neither simple nor obvious.

It involves solving a difficult problem.

In a billiard ball world, described in billiard ball terms, what account can we give of something like consciousness which so obviously is not a billiard ball?—We cannot observe it in others and we cannot explain it in terms of colliding objects, no matter how small the objects. Furthermore, what we know of the workings of the brain (like the processing of incoming patterns of light, and the use of perspectival clues to construct a coherent three-dimensional world) ultimately require an observer i.e. to see the world so-constructed and—*pray tell me*—how does that observer *do their observing?*

Circularity is something of a problem:

It is all too tempting to call upon an inner eye that sees and understands everything, or to have a small, convenient personage secreted inside the cranium (let us call that personage a *homunculus*, and said *homunculus* can perform all the donkey work of making sense of what the brain feeds it, except of course: Dear *Homunculus*, wither thine own *homunculi*?)

Thus we arrive at the aim of this text which is to dig into the key features of consciousness and present a mechanism that delivers consciousness without circularity. This mechanism has to deliver understanding, meaning, moral action and aesthetic appreciation—and yes, it is a mechanism, a sequence of A causes B causes C—a mechanism that delivers consciousness and how thinking, understanding, and our appreciation of three-dimensional space comes about—all without circularity.

The mechanism described here does not have to be the only mechanism and, once understood, it will be seen that any number of variations is possible.

Given the basic mechanism, and elaborations of it that deliver dimensionality, morality and aesthetics, one further consequence will be explored, which is to address the question: *What constitutes a good society?* Thus society will be seen, at its best and finest, to be dependent on our fundamental nature. What we are, and the way we should aspire to be.

The 2025 Updated Edition

THE PRESENT EDITION introduces and starts with a new chapter that presents an important argument that *consciousness is not an emergent property of AI*.

The chapter on The Fair Society is extended to include a discussion of culture as a way to extend a fair society beyond a framework of fixed rules.

A new chapter on the *Nature of Evil* is added, as well as a chapter on how *evolution* might plausibly have delivered the first conscious creatures (which also touches on the *Natural-Unnatural Equivalence Fallacy* and the *Intellectual Fallacy*).

Jack Calverley
June 2025

In this text, the letters MIMH refer to the book "The Man in My Head Has Lost His Mind"; RGBL refer to "This Robot Brain Gets life"; and AIAI refer "Authentic Art in the Age of AI" all by Carter Blakelaw and published by The Logic of Dreams.

Today's AIs Cannot Be Conscious

The Legacy of the Mechanical Turk

A CENTURIES-OLD FRAUD that today's technology should easily (and honestly) outperform is The Case of the Mechanical Turk. Despite the dishonesty, this historic misdemeanour might yet guide enquiry into what lies ahead for AI...

The perpetrator was one Wolfgang von Kempelen. He invented a chess-playing machine, and a great success it was too. The year was 1770 and it was known as The Mechanical Turk. It took the form of a wooden man in a stereotypically Turkish outfit who sat at a cabinet upon which rested a chess board and pieces. The Turk, who had articulated arms and hands, would play against all-comers, and most often win. Sadly, when it came to advancements in artificial intelligence it proved to be a hoax, achieved by concealing a small chess-playing man inside the cabinet. It was he who guided the arms, hands, and head of The Turk.

However the case serves nicely as a metaphor.

The difficulty the small man overcame was the thinking bit. Our Wolfgang had not mastered mechanical thinking so he inserted a small man (let us call that man a *homunculus*) to do it for him.

Today we have chess pretty much licked machine-wise, through micro-electronics, even without the benefits of ChatGPT, Anthropic Claude, or Bing Chat AI (other brands are available).

The problem domain has moved on, or at least expanded in scope and ambition.

We now think of the thinking bit in terms of pattern recognition, classification, speech, three-dimensional modelling, spatial reasoning—driving cars and steering spaceships: heed well Wolfgang!—and of course generating content while, all the time, we seek to replicate and improve upon our own personal thinking machines, to wit: our brains.

Of course the brain does more than mere mechanical thinking: it elevates the content of the thinking to a perceptual level; we are conscious creatures. And we might do well to ask how close a thinking machine can come to replicate our kind of thinking without perception. Here, I take 'perception' to mean feeling stuff: from pain, through taste and smell and the sounds and meanings of words; from understanding Einstein to the stomach-lurch one gets when speeding over a humpback bridge. By contrast I take 'mechanical thinking' to mean—if I dare venture a snappy catch-all—manipulating symbols.

For the purposes of this piece, *mind*, I take to be all and only our conscious experience; *brain*, I take to be the biological mass that lies mainly inside the cranium, and possibly extends to and includes our sense organs.

Professor Richard Gregory (we're talking the mid-1960s and onward) presented us with visual illusions that are indicative of the way the brain interprets visual cues on its way to constructing models of reality inside our heads. Illusions, he argued, are illustrative of how our brains work because in illusions our brains interpret the cues incorrectly, which is taken as evidence they are doing some kind of interpreting in the first place.

And where does perception fit into all this?

When we observe a three-dimensional object, for instance a chess piece, let us say a knight, viewed at an angle, we perceive more or less what arrives at the backs of our eyes which is a two-dimensional pattern, though we appreciate the pattern belongs to a three-dimensional object.

Supposedly, our brains use Gregory's visual cues, which for the most part belong to the two-dimensional pattern (shape, line, shadow and so on, no doubt aided by binocular vision), to infer the object is three-dimensional, and our brains construct an internal model of the object to match this inference. Thus we come to understand the object we perceive (the knight) has depth.

But how does our perceiving-self interpret the chess piece as having depth unless the perceiving-self repeats the process of inference from the two-dimensional pattern, since the pattern is all that we—that is, our perceiving-selves—have to go on?

(Unlike the two dimensions of an image, we do not directly perceive the third dimension, we can only infer it.)

This is the problem of the homunculus. We need a small personage inside our heads to do the perceptual donkey work. And that small personage will need a small personage of their own to do similar donkey work for them, and so on...

Which is to say: to understand consciousness we must not only explain how simple sensation, or feeling, comes about, but also solve the problem of the homunculus; the inner eye; the whatever that experiences our complex world as a complex world—the problem of how, exactly, consciousness in its totality delivers what it does.

And today, when it comes to consciousness, a claim often heard is that at a sufficient level of complexity artificial intelligence will become conscious (solving both problems: sensation and the homunculus); consciousness will prove to be an emergent property of the systems that constitute these mechanistic intelligences—as the conscious mind (the argument must go) is for the brain.

But, Evolution

IF ANIMAL SPECIES developed consciousness as a necessary part of their evolution, then consciousness must deliver an evolutionary advantage. For consciousness to deliver an evolutionary advantage, it must play a causal role in the brain/mind complex; consciousness must make a difference.

Alternatively, if evolution played no selective role, consciousness might be an accidental side-effect or inconsequential variance in the attributes of a species. Or else it might be intrinsic to some microscopic process, and always present, necessarily, but without further consequence (more of these non-selected-for possibilities later).

For now, we might reasonably assume that at some stage in evolution animals evolved to benefit from consciousness. It is not an unreasonable assumption because, for instance, pain delivers a piquancy that outperforms any numerical system of warnings; by being felt, pain presents an incentive that extends beyond mere number.

Emergent Properties

THE AI COMPLEXITY theorists would have it that consciousness is an emergent property; when a system doing brain-like things exceeds some measure of complexity that system becomes conscious.

Emergent properties are familiar to us in various scientific endeavours.

Surface tension is an emergent property.

It's an effect we can observe at the interface between a body of water and a body of air. It is useful to some insects and we can measure it, describe it in terms of resistance, or pressure, or whatever other macroscopic properties.

At the same time we know about water molecules. We know about the bonds between them. We can talk of forces, energy levels, lowest energy states, and so on. All of which can be used to explain surface tension. We have two independent descriptions of one and the same phenomenon. One set of properties (macroscopic) is not obviously a result of the other set of properties (microscopic) unless you do the mathematics. However ultimately, the mathematics—and the science—gives a full account of the macroscopic in terms of the microscopic. A causal chain of events could in principle be established to account for all the observed properties.

If Consciousness Offers a Survival Advantage

IF THE MIND and brain share one and the same, identical, mechanism, as they must if mind is an emergent property of the brain, then any activity in the mind can be wholly accounted for by activity in the brain.

But we have already suggested that if we evolved to have consciousness, then being conscious contributes causally (i.e. adds) to the operation of the brain; the brain would not operate the same way without it. Yet if consciousness is an emergent property of the brain we must be able (in principle) to trace all our conscious behaviour completely, exclusively, and causally in terms of brain activity; consciousness cannot play any additional causal role.

Thus we must conclude: if consciousness is the product of evolution it cannot be an emergent property.

However there is one loophole in this argument which needs addressing.

We have talked of a causal connection between mind and brain delivering a survival advantage, but causal need not be in terms of data or behaviour (as for instance conveyed by signals between neurons). Causal, as with surface tension, might relate to optimum levels of energy.

Possibly, when a creature is awake, its being conscious reduces the energy profile of the brain from which that consciousness emerges. An evolutionary advantage is achieved by being conscious not by altering a creature's behaviour but by delivering the brain to a lower energy state. Lower energy consumption would confer the survival advantage (and consciousness itself might indeed be emergent).

However, this possibility can be dismissed by a thought experiment.

Suppose we build a digital computer that relies on the two lowest energy states of some chosen electron to be its operational 1s and 0s. Let us implement our brain-like system in all its complexity on this computer (in hardware or software, as convenient). If consciousness is an emergent property and consciousness delivers the system that implements it to a lower energy state, since this system cannot operate the same way functionally in any lower energy state than it already does, it cannot become conscious. Consciousness could not be said to be an emergent property of a complex system in such a case; at least one other factor is involved.

Thus either consciousness evolved (plays a separate causal role), or consciousness is an emergent property of biological/mechanical systems blessed with the right kind of complexity, but not both.

If Consciousness Is Accidental and Inconsequential

WE SUGGESTED EARLIER that consciousness might happen to be an accidental, inconsequential, emergent side-effect of the working brain, or simply an inconsequential mutation in the brain itself, neither of which offer any survival advantage.

However if we can demonstrate that being conscious involves an energy or resource overhead, i.e. an evolutionary disadvantage, then consciousness must deliver an additional benefit to outweigh that disadvantage; therefore is causal; therefore is not emergent.

One such demonstration we might call The Argument from the Homunculus.

The mechanism of the brain solves the problem of the homunculus. Which is to say, the brain has a way of avoiding the need for an infinite regress of homunculi for us to make sense of the world. Defeating the homunculus (as will be shown below) requires additional neural circuitry and can only serve consciousness, not the brain, costing any creature doing so energy and resources, and placing the creature at a survival disadvantage unless a greater, other advantage is achieved i.e. by its achieving consciousness.

(And we know the problem of the homunculus is solved, from personal experience.)

Consciousness might be accidental but it is not inconsequential because the brain solves the problem of the homunculus, which has a cost that must be recouped through survival advantage.

If Consciousness Is Intrinsic to Every Brain Cell

WE ALSO SUGGESTED above that consciousness might be "intrinsic to some microscopic process, and always present, necessarily, but without further consequence". However if this is the case then clearly it is not an emergent property arising from the complexity of the system. Consciousness might be present in every neuron (or other brain cell, or in the interactions between brain cells), but these are the building blocks of the complexity of the brain. The point being: if consciousness resides cell-by-cell at cell level, it is not an emergent property of the complexity of the system.

~

The Homunculus: A Reductionist View of Consciousness

THE PROBLEM OF the homunculus is exemplified by the problem of explaining our appreciation of the three-dimensional world.

To repeat our earlier question:

"How does our perceiving-self interpret the chess piece as having depth unless the perceiving-self repeats the process of inference from the two-dimensional pattern, since the pattern is all that we, that is, our perceiving-selves, have to go on?"

The goal of the exercise is to show how our apparently thinking awareness can be constituted from simple components of felt experience—from fragments of colour or sound or smell that themselves perform no thinking at all; they are merely felt; there is nothing beyond them; in fact, they do not even constitute a thinking machine because there can be no homunculus doing any understanding at all —the universe has nothing to offer beyond simple felt experience on that side of the equation. The buck stops here. So, how is that possible? When we have explained that, we will indeed have got rid of the homunculus.

The key to the question (with apologies to the objectivists among you) is to examine our own personal experience; we have superlative access when it comes to the question of what consciousness is like.

Furthermore, and tipping our hats to René Descartes more than to Sigmund Freud, a good starting point is the nature of dreams.

A serious point about dreams is that the content of our dreams can be wildly untrue and yet we accept it without question: Uncle Charles is a rabbit; Aunt Celeste is a badger; I live in a penthouse...

In the dream these things are accepted without question. Only later, when I am awake, I think how bizarre! (and what can it all mean?)

The point is that the brain is quite capable of (and therefore has a mechanism for) conveying to whatever consciousness exists during the dream: 'this scenario or artefact makes perfect sense', 'all is well', 'don't worry about it', 'accept whatever at face value'.

Holding that thought, let us turn to what we perceive. Visually, we perceive broadly the same pattern of light as is incident on the retina. But we do not believe that our perceptions are generated in the retina. Our perceptions are mediated by the brain.

What does the brain add? It tries to make sense of the world about us. It enriches what would otherwise be raw experience. Importantly also, the 'predictive brain' anticipates our impact on the world and plays a role in, for instance, motor control. And it is obvious that we can and do perform simple anticipatory tasks like predicting the flight of a ball in a ball-game in order to catch the ball.

We do not however enjoy a running commentary or labelling as we navigate the world; our experience is not one of augmented reality. Instead most of our visual field, especially the periphery, is gifted with a feeling of 'don't worry about it'.

As I walk along a path in the woods, I do not spend my time worrying about the trees to either side. Nor does my brain generate a running commentary of tree types, of their observable features, or of their evolutionary history. We might go so far as to say that while I continue to be aware of the trees, I pretty much ignore them. The brain is playing the same trick on me in waking life as it does in my dreams with the exception that these perceptions are rooted in the signals coming from my eyes and supported by my other waking senses.

If we accept this version of events we have removed a large burden of what the homunculus has to do. Anything that is peripheral has been taken care of (by the brain, which tells us not to worry). What is left centres on our focus of attention: that part of our visual field that we are, from one moment to the next, actively thinking about.

And here we can draw once again on personal experience (and once again apologise to the objectivists among you). Not only do our brains anticipate what is going to happen, but our own experience is of a world that transitions smoothly, by and large, from one moment to the next. However, perceptions (colours, sounds, smells and so on) are generated by the brain; they come from the brain—by a mechanism yet to be identified—but not from the world around us. So it is our brains that construct the transitions and make them smooth (from the now, through the anticipated, to the fully confirmed next—illusions notwithstanding); our brains see to it that we do not inhabit a jumpy stop-frame animation.

Smoothness might be achieved by gradually replacing infinitesimally small components-of-perception with components of different values, or by morphing the values of extant components-of-perception.

The former 'fading' solution allows that the current world view and the anticipated world view are both present in some measure from moment to moment (and does not require any perceptual calculus). The anticipatory work done by the brain both highlights unexpected change at the earliest opportunity and usefully contributes to our perceived experience by helping to maintain the integrity of objects in the field of view. Furthermore, 'fading' offers us an account of how we perceive the third dimension. We part-perceive what is going to happen; how the world is going to change; how a three-dimensional object will reveal itself. The third dimension is the ghost of what might happen next (at a stretch, for those fond of irony, you might say: we derive space from time).

(NB 'fading' does not imply a synchronous mechanism, merely that the old, the anticipated, and the new overlap in some way.)

The upshot is; our homunculus has been robbed of yet another task. We no longer require it to make sense of the third dimension; we are okay with the two dimensions we already have.

The exploration can be pursued further, and elsewhere in this volume we offer ways to understand imagination, speech, and meaning, as also: how to appreciate the intricate feelings that accompany art and morality—all without recourse to a homunculus.

For the purposes of the present chapter, in order to support the titular claim, ideally we would want to show that defeating the homunculus involves specific brain circuitry that is not otherwise needed but which would consume both energy and resources. The prime candidate for this mechanism would be the brain circuitry that performs perceptual fading. The brain does more than perform a simple comparison between anticipation and actuality—

which is all it would need to alert it to unexpected change in the world. There is no reason, nor benefit, to the brain's having a fading mechanism, nor to developing it in the first place.

For consciousness, 'fading' aids clarity, providing delineation and continuity to the things we perceive. This in turn serves the causal story for consciousness via the localisation of e.g. pain, when consciousness makes its causal difference to the creature that bears it (as is elaborated in other chapters).

While all the above makes the case for the title of this chapter, the defeat of the homunculus both points to how the content of perception is arrived at, and offers a separate elaboration of how consciousness is not an emergent property of a 'sufficiently complex system'.

In defeating the homunculus we have arrived at a mechanism—an interface if you will—that requires only simple sensations (colour, sound, smell etc.) to complete it. Simple sensations can be a simple property of the universe, and so long as we can combine simple sensations through some kind of field effect, to unify the whole into a contiguous individual self, no further explanation is required.

Consciousness is seen to be other than the biological brain (or machine) that generates its content.

Indeed, the go-to claim of consciousness might be: the piquancy of pain is beyond number because consciousness is something other than process or calculation.

We started by suggesting the Mechanical Turk might yet guide enquiry into what lies ahead for AI.

We have arrived at the position where AIs will only gain consciousness if we design it in—if we replicate that specific component of a biological system that captures sensation.

Thus, if AIs become conscious, it will not be an accident, but oh what troubled possibilities we will then face!

IN THE MEANTIME the rest of this text elaborates how consciousness comes about without being part of the biological brain that generates the content.

Step One – *Perceptions and the Brain*

Preamble A:

IN EVERYDAY DISCOURSE about our experience, the *content* of perception—the pale blue of a region of sky, the tone of the bass guitar in the beat of a dance track, or the sweet almond flavour of marzipan—*might* be thought of as distinct from the *perceiving* since I can choose where I focus my attention: on the view through a restaurant window, on the music coming from the cafe opposite, or on the marzipan coating of the slice of Battenberg cake I am eating.

However, let us for the purpose of this enquiry start by treating the content of perception and our experiencing that perception—the *perceiving*, as it were—as inseparable. There is no content without the experience; there is no experience without the content. For our purposes, the *perceiving* is distinct from the deliberate, or otherwise, *action* of setting the focus of one's attention here or there—on the cake or on the music.

Preamble B:

IT IS ULTIMATELY an aggregation of these content/perceiving pairings that constitutes the totality of our conscious awareness. Which is to say that any other aspect of our brain's conscious processes: the focussing of attention, acts of will, or anger, greed and so on must either be incorporated into the scheme as content/perceiving pairings themselves, or be explicable in terms of some arrangement of content/perceiving pairings.

Which is to say, there is nothing in our consciousness beyond these content/perceiving pairings so every conscious experience must be capable of expression in terms of some or other, or set of content/perceiving pairings.

Preamble C:

SINCE THE WORD 'perceiving' is too easily confused with action, my preference will be to use the word 'experience' when emphasising the *perceiving* side of the content/perceiving pairing. In what follows the words 'perception', 'sensation', 'feeling' and 'consciousness', unless otherwise qualified, refer to some arrangement of content/experience pairings. And a 'mind' refers to the sum total of an individual's consciousness, while a 'brain' refers to the sum total of the biological mass of an individual that gives rise to their consciousness.

Preamble D:

IF THIS STARTING point is wrong-headed, the following enquiry should reveal how and why it is wrong-headed and offer an alternative view and better explanation of the nature of consciousness. In particular we can expect our notion of the content/experience pairings will be refined. And because of this starting point and direction of travel, you might call the enquiry *reductionist*. The question is: can the approach be shown to work? I submit that it can.

Idea:

PERCEPTIONS BELONG TO the brain, are generated by the brain, are private to the brain, exist only within the brain, and do not extend into the external world beyond our bodies.

Elaboration:

THE SKY IS not blue. Rather: photons of light of certain frequencies arrive on the backs of our eyes from the atmosphere. Light receptor cells in our eyes then send electro-chemical signals into the brain, and the brain generates the sensation of some or other colour in response to the electro-chemical signals.

The air around us does not carry the sound of a whistle. A whistle when blown generates a compression wave in the air and sustains a certain frequency which impinges on sensitive hairs in the ear. A subset of the sensitive hairs vibrates in resonance to the frequency of the compression wave and initiates electro-chemical signals that travel along neurons into the brain, whereupon the brain generates the sensation of a sound—in this case the continuous tone that we recognise derives from a whistle.

Our perceptions are generated by our brains; we do not swim in a sea of perceptions picking up those useful to us as we pass through them (or them through us).

Corollary:

AT FIRST BLUSH, the perceptions described here accord with the philosophical concept of Secondary Qualities.

Step Two – *Inferring Three Dimensional Space*

Idea:

THE THREE-DIMENSIONAL world of objects we see and feel, with the apparent locations of sounds, and our three-dimensional experience of our own bodies, is all generated by the brain. This generated three-dimensional world is the brain's best guess as to what the world is like. An assembly of perceptions, featuring a notional self at the centre, is the most convenient and efficient way the brain possesses to gather and express its best guess about the world.

Elaboration:

THE BRAIN INFERS the three-dimensional nature of the world from the signals it receives from the senses, and it generates perceptions that are both consistent with its inferences, as well as being a good fit to the sensory data.

For example, the brain grasps that a brick is a three-dimensional block (inferred without the aid of consciousness from angles and lines and so on in signals coming from the eyes) and the brain generates a two-dimensional array of colour perceptions to represent the brick, i.e. roughly matching whatever pattern of light impinges on, and can be corroborated by, those signals arriving from the backs of the eyes.

(Exactly how the three-dimensional aspect is conveyed to consciousness is discussed in a later Step—consciousness consists only of content/experience pairs; we cannot have a second brain, an inner eye, or a *homunculus* to interpret our

14

array of content/experience pairs. To offer such an explanation would be circular and question-begging and no explanation at all.)

Broadly, the brain only generates perceptions that correspond to signals coming from the senses. These perceptions correspond reliably enough that we are used to asserting: "But I can see such-and-such," "I can hear such-and-such," and so on. This is not to deny that errors—e.g. hallucinations—can occur, and often do. It is only to say that to interact effectively with the world the brain must be correct more often than not; the internal model it builds must for the most part correspond to those aspects of the world that it can habitually verify by further exploration and are useful to it for survival.

The brain can and will make *incorrect* inferences (in terms of its three-dimensional modelling): what at first appears to be a rock, might turn out to be a sheep settled in long grass chewing cud.

The brain can and will generate *incorrect* perceptions (for what we roughly label secondary qualities): the words of a song might be heard incorrectly; a shadow on a wall might turn out to be a *trompe l'oeil*.

The brain does its best to be accurate, but it will manufacture additional content (both in constructing the model and in generating perceptions) and go on to fill in any gaps and override uncertainty in sensory data to complete the perceptual picture it presents of the world when a majority of sensory evidence indicates the likely existence of what the brain now infers.

When generating perceptions, the brain generates meaningful content—content that is useful and usable when it comes to interacting with the world. This extends beyond mere perceptual appearance. For instance, it is useful to know that a rock is a rock i.e. a single aggregate of hard material that can be treated as one particular item in the world.

The fact that a set of visual perceptions happens to constitute *a rock* must be available to the conscious whole, i.e. as supplementary information. To be complete, the account of consciousness we arrive at must include an account of how this additional information is available to consciousness, i.e. experienced. (i.e. what does a brain do that would not be achieved by simply generating perceptions directly, without intervention, in the light receptors at the back of the eye?)

Corollary:

AT FIRST BLUSH, the three-dimensional model generated by the brain accords to the philosophical concept of Primary Qualities.

Step Three – *Maximise Meaning*

Idea:

THE BRAIN HAS limited flexibility in terms of the perceptions it generates. In this respect, it is a machine dedicated to a single task. It is pre-configured to maximise meaning and to organise the perceptions it generates in a manner that is consistent with that meaning.

Elaboration:

WORDS IN A language familiar to us are perceived fully formed, as recognised, individual words, but words from an unknown language arrive as jumbled sounds.

It is hard work to listen to the sounds that make up words we recognise. The brain naturally escalates informational content to the maximum meaning it can. Moreover it is difficult to un-see, for instance, a fox in the woods once you have seen it; you can't fully un-see it unless you realise it was actually just a dog, or a piece of wood, and you made a mistake.

Meaning in this context encompasses all the additional understanding the brain can bring to some specific aspect of the world. This additional understanding must be available (yet to be elaborated) to the perceptual whole (the sum total of content/experience pairs) that the brain generates.

If the brain does not recognise some set of sensory data, it generates raw, uninterpreted perceptions of colour, sound etc.

It is possible by effort and skill, and by an act of will, to get the brain to generate the raw component percepts of an item for which a meaningful perception has been generated, for instance the sounds that make up a word if one re-considers the word as a sample of a regional accent one wants to reproduce in one's own speech.

It is possible also, intentionally, to impose a new context on an existing perception, and the brain can flip its interpretation (such as in optical illusions).

Corollary:

ALTHOUGH THE BRAIN generates its own world view, we cannot choose to invent any world we like. The brain operates automatically and for the most part without conscious control to generate a model of the world that best fits data from the senses (receiving data both directly and via memory). It is in the nature of the brain to minimise inconsistencies across its world view—i.e. the world view it generates as perceptions. You cannot simply create, generate, or believe what you want about the world. That would be to confuse the brain's unconscious and efficient process of generating a world view with the mind's emotional and wilful (imagination-based and possibly fantastical and possibly pathological) desire for things to be other than they are.

Step Four – *The Homunculus Must Go*

Idea:

THE THREE-DIMENSIONAL world inferred by the brain from the senses, and re-presented in the perceptions that the brain generates, must contain all its own understanding. We cannot introduce a second brain, or mind, to make sense of either the inferred three-dimensional model or the associated assemblage of perceptions. To do so would be to beg the question *What Makes Us Conscious?* Which is to say, understanding and meaning must be integral to being conscious and exist only within the confines of consciousness.

Elaboration:

THIS IDEA IS exemplified by the idea of a *homunculus*.

For our purposes a *homunculus* reminds us of a small man concealed inside an apparently smart machine doing the smart things that otherwise, from an external point of view, are attributed to the miraculous machine.

The brain/mind must understand itself. It would be question-begging to add something else and new and separate from the brain/mind that performs the understanding.

If we had a *something*—a process or device or etherial presence—'scanning' the brain/mind's internal, dynamic three-dimensional model, we would still have to explain how that *something* worked. Alternatively, if we had a *something* 'scanning' and interpreting a notional two-dimensional cinema screen of perceptions, and making sense of the cinema screen, we would have to explain how that *something* works. In other words, how does the *homunculus* understand anything?

Notice that the cinema screen is notionally the same as the image on the back of the eye. But perceptions are not generated in the retina; perceptions are manufactured by the brain which also does the job of associating shapes etc. with the things they 'mean' (colloquially, *what they are*). In this sense the brain's role is to 'add meaning' to raw sensory data and 'to make sense of' the world in so far as the world impinges upon the senses.

Step Five - *Meaning(M)*

Idea:

WE CAN AVOID having to introduce a homunculus by allowing the notional cinema screen of content/experience pairs to include content/experience pairs other than those directly and obviously corresponding to the senses.

Elaboration:

WHEN, FROM SECOND to second, the brain constructs its assemblage of content/experience pairs as we go about our daily lives, we are not aware of every detail, every fact, name, history or whatever that goes with those things that are represented in the notional cinema screen of perception.

We do not inhabit an augmented reality world where everything about us is labelled. We do not walk a footpath and enjoy an ongoing commentary of everything all the time: 'there's a yellow stone' 'there's a black stone' 'there's a patch of blue sky—and that's because of light scattered off atomic oxygen...' etc. etc. There would not be enough time to enumerate all we know, and explain, and to vocalise and in each moment to comprehend every available item in our perceptual field. For the most part we simply accept most of the content of that field as being 'natural' and 'expected' and 'of no great surprise'.

Only when a butterfly crosses our path, and attracts our attention, do we focus on it and say to ourselves (perhaps)

"Is that a peacock, or a red admiral? It's very bright whatever it is, but I can never remember which is which."

So let us give an account of those things in the assemblage of content/experience pairs (the notional cinema screen) that we are unworried about—the majority of stuff—leaving us to focus on the difficult bits.

Here it is useful to think about dreams because they present this feature of 'not being worried about the way the world is' in notable, strange abundance.

We simply accept the contents of a dream, regardless how wild it may seem when reflected upon once we awaken. The thing (whatever incongruity it happened to be) seemed so *natural* and *apt* and *in its right place* in the dream world at the time of the dream.

This lack of worry (one might even say *disinterest*) in the vast majority of those things that constitute the cinema screen of content/experience pairs can be accommodated in that cinema screen by a new kind content/experience pair that does not correspond to any one particular sense organ (although you might say, for these purposes, 'the brain is the sense organ in question'), but which conveys the sensation of 'not having to worry about this portion of the perceptual field'. This is what Blakelaw refers to as the 'qualia of Meaning(M)' which he elaborates as 'the feeling that this content is adequate'[1]. The brain has identified the object: stone, sky, grass, tree, bird, or whatever it is; the object presents no new threat or interest; the brain could elaborate if called upon to do so, but flags this thing as 'in its right place in the world'.

Given such content/experience pairs of Meaning(M), and distributing them widely across the notional cinema screen of perception, we can see that the brain knows unconsciously much more than we need to hold at any one time in our field of consciousness.

Importantly for us, introducing qualia of Meaning(M) deprives the homunculus of a whole load of work. A large part of our perceptual field is pervaded by this new feeling of 'un-worry'.

---

1 RBGL Chapter 9. Blakelaw's qualia correspond loosely to our content/experience pairs.

Step Six – *An Argument from Energy*

Idea:

CONSCIOUSNESS IS REAL. It exists, at least for me, when I assert that it exists. It is thus, at the very least, at those times, a thing in the universe.

Consciousness comes and goes. There must be a change in some other aspect of the universe that makes at least these two transitions happen[2]. Any change that induces these transitions must involve energy of some kind.

Furthermore, whatever causal role we may ascribe to it, consciousness interacts with the physical world, at the very least to the extent that the brain governs the content of experience.

We take the physical world to be made up of fundamental particles (quarks, photons, electrons, and so on). The candidates for the mechanism whereby consciousness comes about are such as: special

---

2 Even if consciousness shuts itself down that would ultimately be in response to starting itself up. And in dissipation or whatever, the energy must go somewhere, be conserved, or be re-absorbed into the fabric of the universe in some explicable/ consistent/coherent way (the universe operates reliably, which means consistently as if following a rule or principle) Footnote 2: There is an implied first event in the universe, indeed an implied need for every event to belong to a causal chain. Later it will be seen that this is only partially true; random (apparently un- caused) disturbances are allowed, indeed necessary, and not all of them need initiate a causal chain of events, though some do, and a chain, once initiated, must play through to its causal end. I don't think this in controversial: quantum noise being one such instance

arrangements of physical particles and changes in those arrangements (including e.g. emergence), *or* transitions in the states and energy levels of those particles, *or* interactions between particles of different kinds. Interactions, transitions, or establishing particular arrangements all involve energy (although the concept of emergence needs more elaboration). Even the collapse of a wave function in quantum entanglement involves the energy of the interaction that triggers the collapse.

Since consciousness comes about through an energetic transaction, it must at least for some time appropriate some part of that energy for itself (i.e. the energy from the interaction, process or whatever that brings said consciousness about).

While the energy is transmuted to instantiate[3] consciousness, it is its own distinct form of energy (available to interact with like-energies in some characteristic way).

Blakelaw posits that consciousness is a fundamental property of the universe, meaning we need look no further than this energy field, and the particles that might arise in it, for an explanation of consciousness.

He calls this field the *Gleeon Field* and the particles that it supports *Gleeons*.

Elaboration:

WHILE WE MIGHT simply say that thus-and-such a physical (for instance it might be a charged-particle) event will generate a gleeon. we have then to give an account of the life cycle of the gleeon.

Furthermore, if there is such a gleeon field, with associated particle life-cycles, why have we not witnessed the coming and going of these particles at least in the form of missing energy in collider experiments and so on?

Although in part the answer to this might be that gleeon generation is only possible via structures like the brain (rendering such collider examination difficult, as well as unethical), Blakelaw suggests a different lifecycle for the gleeon which, he argues, serves Nature better, since it is simpler and more efficient.

---

3 trigger and possibly sustain

Blakelaw suggests that particles in the gleeon field pop into and out of existence all the time as quantum noise. But he suggests that these particles do not bear conscious experience. Rather they are pre-conscious. Pre-conscious gleeons have no content—how can they since it is structures such as those in the brain that govern content? What must happen is that activity in the brain captures randomly occurring pre-conscious gleeons (of which there are myriads) and holds them for some duration in a particular energy state or configuration before releasing them back to their pre-conscious state, to decay in the same way as does all other quantum background noise.

The particular energy state or configuration is what determines content.

This is energy-efficient because the brain does not have to generate gleeons.

It also paints a picture of the brain swimming in a sea of pre-conscious gleeons, and helping itself to clouds of millions of them at any one time to constitute a substantial enough and contiguous region of consciousness that we are able to perceive a relatively rich (and in our case complex) world.

This account of gleeon activity is all set to explain sensations of colour, smell, taste, sound frequency, and so on (broadly The Secondary Qualities of Step 1, above) plus Blakelaw's qualia of Meaning(M).

However, our experience of three dimensions, of time, language and of the imagination—indeed the experience of the *Me*-ness of Me—cannot be explained so simply, and yet they must be explicable in terms of content/experience pairs, as will be shown below. Which is to say: there has to be a way of avoiding the *homunculus* mentioned in Step 4.

Consolidation:

WE HAVE MENTIONED the cinema screen of the mind, something akin to the image that is incident on the back of the eye but to which additional meaning is (i) added by the brain and (ii) becomes available as we (the mind/brain) change the focus of our attention.

The cinema screen is akin to what, colloquially, is observed by 'the mind's eye' or processed by the brain's apparent *homunculus*—neither of which provides us with an explanation.

However, we can usefully develop the metaphor of a cinema screen if we allow the screen to be wrap-around, closing us in from every direction, like the inside surface of a hollow sphere. However, we must take care not to assign it to some large-scale physical structure in the brain (none has ever been observed), indeed any physicality it might possess, or correspond to, would have to be fluid and flexible, of no fixed location, shape or size.

The wrap-around cinema screen (Blakelaw calls it *The Surface*) must be capable of generating myriads of content/experience pairs of various kinds. For example, the sounds that our brains generate may appear to come from any direction, whereas the things we see are generated essentially in front of us (notwithstanding imagination, Step 9). The things we smell are generated in a very limited field of sensation, while our sense of our own bodies can exist, at one time or another, in any direction (I can scratch the top of my head or the underside of my foot). Indeed bodily sensations may come multiply from one particular direction (e.g. a thorn in the sole of my foot and an itch behind my knee might form a straight line with my notional centre of perception, which creates a scenario that demands a more complex elaboration in terms of The Surface).

So let us allow that the Surface can come into being in a living brain, and that it arises where brain cells have captured gleeons and stabilised or fixed them with some characteristic energy or configuration complementary to a particular sense organ. In other words, regions of The Surface favour different mixes of content/experience pairings according to the direction they lie in from a notional centre of perception (N.B. ultimately we will have to disavow this notional centre of perception)—with some regions supporting many kinds or pairings, others few.

To re-iterate, the location of The Surface is not fixed in the brain—indeed many Surfaces or partial Surfaces may exist and come and go in the brain during the brain's normal functioning. However, 'We' will notice only those that are capable of sustaining or laying down memories. And it would seem natural to conclude that the brain tends to produce one main complete Surface, as this unified world view is most useful in survival terms[4].

We have said the Surface is like the inside of a hollow sphere. Why the inside? Why not the outside? Indeed what can any such directionality mean in terms of content/experience pairs? If the brain captures and energises a gleeon, what orientation should it have and what can that mean (i.e. what consequence) for consciousness?

In our Me-ness there is a definite sense of 'looking out', a sense of the world being beyond us—even our bodies are 'beyond' our consciousness of them; there is an implicit directionality built into content/experience pairs.

Blakelaw suggests that this directionality comes about uniformly because (i) activated gleeons are directional, and (ii) it takes the least energy to maintain a cloud of gleeons in a spheroidal shell when they all line up as close to parallel as they can and face inward. Thus, given their large numbers, small size, and overall spheroidal arrangement, this means each activated gleeon will tend to align to a radius of the Surface[5]. As to whether gleeons are orientated one way or another along a radius, that too must be a matter of adopting the lowest energy state[6].

In response to Steps 1 to 6 we introduce The Surface, which is a mobile, variably shaped region where gleeons are captured to produce content/experience pairs. We have suggested that this is done in astronomically large numbers, and that gleeons have directionality, and are capable of alignment.

---

4 The left hand needs to 'know' what the right hand is doing.

5 Hence spheroidal. This need not be a perfect sphere, it requires only that the path from any gleeon on The Surface to a notional centre (the implied mind's eye) is unobstructed by other gleeons. There is no mechanism to perceive distance [gleeon-to-gleeon; gleeon-to-centre] within the Surface. Near and far gleeons contribute equally. But we cannot allow two gleeons on the same radius, especially as representative of distance. If we introduce any such representation of distance, we introduce the need for a homunculus.

6 If orientation is a matter of an energy state, it is possible that the arrangement of adjacent gleeons can have a causal impact on the processes that give rise to them; they might generate a motive force on their own source, a backforce, and may even 'resist' [there is an energy cost/threshold to] certain transitions.

The Surface constitutes our awareness of a unified world and for the most part we accept its content without worry or particular attention since the brain generates qualia of Meaning(M) throughout. However this simple passive system of experience does not explain our appreciation of three dimensions nor our cognitions (and recognition) of objects in (say) our field of view, nor indeed how we perform actions and set and achieve goals... and much more besides.

Step Seven – *The Smoothness of the World*

Idea:

OUR MOMENT-TO-MOMENT experience of the world is smooth and contiguous; there are no cinema-style jump cuts (although we might suffer from the occasional surprise).

If the life cycle of a gleeon is from pre-conscious, to content-bearing, and back to pre-conscious, then perceptual transitions in an assembly of gleeons (The Surface) are achieved through changes in the numbers of gleeons bearing some particular content or other. For smooth transitions, for instance from colour A to colour B, the region of the surface in question might initially be fully populated by gleeons bearing the colour A, then gradually A-bearing gleeons return to their pre-conscious state and are replaced by B-bearing gleeons[7].

However the world as we perceive it is more than a series of colours, it is constituted of objects and materials that we can individuate, and these objects and materials can change their location and orientation in our perceptual field independently of us or because we choose to change our location and orientation relative to them. Our perception of these changes is for the most part smooth, meaning that the population of gleeons giving rise to these perceptions does not change abruptly; nor do we find ourselves re-evaluating everything in our perceptual field from one moment to the next as change occurs.

---

7 For Blakelaw gleeons come and go; they do not themselves transition from A-bearing to B-bearing.

The smooth change might come about through time lags in the decay of the gleeons, or because the brain predicts the way the world is about to change and generates anticipatory gleeons in advance of supportive evidence from the senses.

Blakelaw dismisses time lag decays because decays ought all to happen with the same time lag, meaning an explanation of smooth, contiguous transitions is still required, and he favours the anticipatory approach because it has a survival advantage in evolutionary terms, as part of the brain's mechanism for noticing the untoward, which might be a food source, or prey, or a mate. Also, this strategy leverages any processing the brain has already done towards recognising the thing or material, maximising the value of that processing to the individual.

The brain does not merely recognise and assign meaning to the things in the world that impinge on our senses, it also anticipates what those things will do next; a characteristic *behaviour*[8] is assigned to every thing we experience, even if that behaviour relates to how we perceive (say) a block of stone when we walk around it, or when we turn it in our hands.

---

8 The word 'behaviour' is not intended to imply any agency; it is merely convenient shorthand for 'characteristic movement or changes in appearance for any number of a broad range of reasons'.

Step Eight – *Three Dimensions, Motion and Anticipation*

Idea:

HAVING INTRODUCED THE idea of behaviour (in the specific sense of Step 7) we have a way to explain our understanding and experience of three-dimensionality exclusively in The Surface, without having to revert to a homunculus or inner eye or any other additional mechanism (any of which begs the question: how do we perceive depth?).

The brain interprets data coming from the senses and no doubt builds up some kind of three-dimensional model of the world and the objects in it, as might be inferred from lines of perspective, binocular vision, our senses of touch and motion and so on. But we do not perceive this model. What we perceive are aspects of this model which are corroborated by data from the senses (two-dimensionally on The Surface) plus the anticipated behaviours of those objects, e.g. as we or they move in the world, including such small movements as turning our heads. We do not perceive three-dimensionality directly, we are merely unsurprised when three-dimensional objects change their two-dimensional (projected, as it were) shape in our perceptual field.

The third dimension is merely the ghost of what might happen—were we to move, or were the object/material to move, or should either continue to move as they currently are.

It is important to remember that we are not dealing with perceptions from a single sense organ. Our two-dimensional perceptions and their anticipations arise from sight and sound and touch and reach (proprioception) and motion and others besides, which reinforce each other to provide a consistent, coherent experience of the world, albeit without directly experiencing any third dimension. The brain may 'know' the third dimension exists, but we never directly perceive the third dimension, nor do we (as perceiving entities) infer it to any degree whatsoever—to infer it would be to invite the homunculus into our heads, and explanation must stop somewhere; it stops in The Surface. All there is, for us, is The Surface and our confidence in the verisimilitude of its two-dimensional[9] content (via gleeons bearing Meaning(M)) and the smoothness of transitions (meaning the brain's estimation of how the world is and predictions about how the world is changing are correct).

Elaboration:

THE BRAIN (NOT THE MIND) creates a three-dimensional model of its best guess as to the way the world is, based on the limited data coming from the senses. The brain generates perceptions (content/experience pairs or *qualia*) that correspond both to the model and to the limited data from the senses. Where the brain is confident in the identity of the three dimensional objects it has generated, it also supplies qualia of Meaning(M)[10] to the perceptual surface, in the region of the surface corresponding to those objects.

The brain anticipates how objects and materials in the three-dimensional world it has generated are going to move, or change, and weakly injects those anticipations as content/experience pairs into The surface—weakly here meaning 'in low numbers' i.e. low in density compared to the generated model that is currently held to be veridical.

This allows for smooth transitions in perceptual experience and also reflects the fact that the brain has a mechanism for detecting unforeseen change that it has not anticipated, i.e. from threats or opportunities in the world,

---

9 Strictly speaking not two-dimensional since it is spherical, but it is a surface.

10 Qualia of Meaning(M) convey nothing more than a feeling of confidence—they have no informational content beyond the implicit confidence.

which it makes overt through perceptions (a benefit in terms of causality and free will as discussed later).

We do not perceive the three dimensional model created by the brain.

Rather, the brain creates perceptions (content/experience pairs) in the form of The Surface based on that model. The Surface is one and the same as our experience. It would be wrong even to say 'we perceive The Surface'. In this respect any talk of the kind 'we perceive' is immediately misleading. We do not perceive; we are our perceptions. 'We' (each of us, and all creatures capable of creating surfaces to any degree) are both the experiencing thing and the content of that experience. Separating the two creates the problem of the *homunculus* or inner-eye. A gleeon that has been captured by the brain is both content and experience.

The most obvious difficult problems that have to be addressed, and explained, are how dimensionality and how language are possible when perception is, to all intents and purposes a Flat Now. Above we have given an account of how our world is intuitively[11] understood by us as three-dimensional. An account of language is saved for a later step.

---

11 Which is to say, before we learn perspective drawing or maths.

Step Nine - *Imagination and Action*

Idea:

WHEN I IMAGINE something, the brain weakly generates content/experience pairs that correspond to that thing, placing those content/experience pairs wherever it is the brain has decided the thing needs locating in the world.

I might imagine my hand, fingers, thumb, palm, palm-print, fingernails, wrinkles and so on behind my head where I cannot directly see it, or them. This means that visual qualia may be generated in any location across The Surface, although of course the maximum capacity for visual qualia generation must exist wherever the brain might generate qualia for the visual field that corresponds to data directly from the eyes.

The same can be said of hearing[12], pain and proprioception, although it is questionable whether we experience smell as coming from anywhere other than our nasal passages (or taste from the possible positions of the tongue), and feelings such as love and rage seem to permeate the whole of our beings, suggesting they in some way act only across the whole Surface, or not at all, which will need further elaboration (later in this text).

---

12 The source of a sound is a fluid thing; the brain tends to force the sound onto the object it guesses is the source, which often is not the case; here the brain relies more on its model than it does on data from the ears, which of course is merely stereo (albeit perhaps interpreted by deconvolution of patterns created by flesh of our ears—but that kind of consideration is beyond the remit of this text).

Only in dreams, or in hallucinatory states, do the qualia of the brain's imagined world achieve a strength of density comparable to that normally achieved during the brain's daytime 'veridical' activity.

Similarly for physical actions. Our brains can imagine where a limb could be and should be, but currently is not, and stimulate the muscles of the body so that the position of the limb changes until it adopts the aimed-for position.

This mechanism for imagined things easily extends to mental feats like arithmetic (on an imagined blackboard) or chess moves or other puzzle-solving.

Ultimately in many cases, of course, a mechanism such as this is subsumed into a conditioned response and we solve such problems automatically; what had taken 'conscious effort' is done 'without a second thought' i.e. the mechanism goes unperceived, except, perhaps, the final impulse to move the body this way or that[13].

---

13 Including speech acts, even characteristic psychological patterns of behaviour—X never has a nice word to say...

Step Ten - *Speech*

Idea:

SPEECH INVOLVES A series of sounds over an extended period of time and yet we have characterised The Surface as *The Flat Now*. If The Surface operates only in the moment (or at least sustains some particular state only for the duration of the gleeons comprising that state), what account can we give of a series of sounds, and their meanings, that constitute words and extend over time?

A word does not arrive all at once. It is a variable noise that has some duration and the brain plays that noise into the surface as a recognised, meaningful word.

Of course, the brain does the understanding, and can merely flag the word or words as having Meaning(M)—nothing to worry about here—while delivering the more or less complicated sounds of them to the Surface.

And yet we hear words; we do not hear sounds.

I hear an instrument playing; I do not hear noise.

Furthermore, understanding the words must be more than generating Meaning(M) whenever they are played into The Surface (understanding is a different kind of meaning).

Words and music (phrasings or parts thereof, down to a note on an oboe) appear to be whole because the brain anticipates the sound of them and delivers the anticipation into the Surface in the same way that behaviours are anticipated and deliver our experience of three-dimensionality i.e. in respect of spacial objects.

And yet every word seems to have its own sound, which has a unity in itself, and is recognisable, and is more than for instance, the blast noise of someone blowing a raspberry.

It is however an error to think we should be looking for a new sound: it is not that the word has some special sound, rather it is that we no longer pay attention to the actual sound of it. It loses the detail of its sound because we understand it, and have no need of the noise. A recognised word is a lesser sound than an unrecognised word. It is more shape than content.

There is still the question of how meaning (as in understanding) is captured by the brain and conveyed to The Surface.

It would seem that the brain parses sentences as they arrive, builds up enough of a picture as it needs (i.e. some kind of unconscious mental model of what might make a sentence true, even for nonsense sentences) leaving understanding as largely implicit and not experienced in The Surface unless we have to 'think about what X has just said' in which case we are invited to imagine in The Surface the scenarios in which the words just spoken are true.

The words "Sharon has thrown the ball at the dog" can be understood just as much as "Churchill's influence on Thatcher was not inconsiderable" or "Relativity is not compatible with Quantum Mechanics".

The brain, as always, is alert to the unknown, the unfamiliar, and the potential threat. In some sense it only half-listens to the familiar and often focus in The Surface need not be particularly sharp. "Sharon throws a ball..." I get it. I know what you're saying. I don't have to imagine it in detail, or question Sharon's motives, let's move on...

Step Eleven - *Time*

Idea:

WE DO NOT perceive the flow of time. As mentioned before, any talk of 'our perceiving' immediately muddies the waters and creates the problem of a thing separate from the perceiving that is doing the perceiving.

The Surface changes over time.

The Surface is also capable of receiving ratiocinations from the brain, which the brain asserts are true, for instance linguistic ratiocinations or real or imagined clock faces which offer explanations of Time, and of the passage of time, to all of which the brain confers truth, or endorses with Meaning(M) but The Surface does not 'perceive time'.

Change occurs and transitions are smooth so that the world seems contiguous.

But for all I know I might be in a simulation which not merely clocks forward one machine/processor clock once per external-world millennium, but in fact varies its clock cycle. Sometimes the external-world microsecond, sometimes the external world hour, sometimes the external world millennium. So long as the brain feeds The Surface, and The Surface does not decay between times ,'I' would not know the difference. The brain/mind believes itself, and the brain operates such that, The Surface might include/encompass on occasion talk or thoughts about Time, and the passage of time, yet all there is is The Now and a faint anticipation of what is to come.

(See also the piece: "Time is the Ghost of the Next Thing That Might Happen".)

Step Twelve - *Free Will*

Idea:

CONSCIOUSNESS FOLLOWS THE brain activity that creates it; we become conscious of decisions up to half a second after the brain has taken them. So how are our conscious thoughts and conscious actions not determined in advance of our having them and doing them? Are we not therefore devoid of free will, our consciousnesses being deprived of agency, and merely 'tagged on' after the fact?

Blakelaw argues that we do act freely and that we act in response to our needs and desires in a given context but these actions could, in principle, be calculated in advance because our brains do not act randomly. Furthermore consciousness plays a causal role in the decision-making but it does not have the immediacy of the "do this here now!" kind.

Elaboration:

BLAKELAW ARGUES THAT consciousness must offer an evolutionary advantage and therefore must play a causal role in our conduct in the world. If causality is from the brain to The Surface, with a time delay, then causality must be not in the moment so much as in the memory. i.e. Activity in The Surface, strength of feeling, appreciation of pain, and so on must be laid down in some form of memory and inform future behaviour, as enacted by the brain.

We can, therefore, through experience and by contemplation[14] change our behaviour. Thus consciousness makes a difference.

But still this does not leave us arbitrarily free.

'free will' is sometimes taken as meaning the same as 'conscious choice'.

Blakelaw paints a picture whereby we are free to conduct ourselves as we wish (within the limits of real-world physics and provided we are not physically constrained) but that this is predictable, and our conduct might be viewed as determinable, except that the world is not pre-determined.

Moreover, Blakelaw would have it, we are reliable machines that have insulated ourselves against e.g. random quantum fluctuations[15], so we will behave reliably, as we wish, but in an in-principle determinable way, except the world we inhabit is not pre-determined because it is not 'designed' (through evolution) to be free from randomness (as per quantum fluctuations) indeed the world we inhabit benefits from such randomness because, ultimately a greater number of possible events, scenarios and situations can play out, such that an optimum physical reality can develop.

We are free; our conduct is as we wish it and also entirely, in principle, predictable (would not have been otherwise)[16], given some circumstance or other in Nature; however the circumstances presented to us by Nature are not predictable nor pre-determined.

---

14 Not contemplation in the sense of wilfully considering, we cannot insert a sui generis free will by sleight of hand, but in the sense of re-remembering and reinforcing particularly potent memories.

15 While gleeons arrive via random quantum fluctuations, they occur in such large numbers that laws apply to their en-mass behaviour much as the laws of thermodynamics arise from the en-mass behaviour of enormous numbers of individually pretty much randomly directed atoms or molecules.

16 It is to our and Nature's benefit that what it produces is robust... genetic choices must work, be effective and be reliable, otherwise a different mechanism is needed and would be found to deliver change and the survival of the species.

Step Thirteen - *Love and Rage, Locality and the Field*

Idea:

SOME SENSATIONS CORRESPOND 'geographically' to the organ that detects them, like pain; others give rise to sensations anywhere in the surface, like sound, whereas love and rage are visceral, seeming to arise, generally, from the musculature of the torso.

Nonetheless, The Surface presents a unity of whole. Which is to say the blue of the sky might be adjacent to the green of the grass but importantly they belong to the same whole experience. The blue of my sky is adjacent the green of my grass.

And how is that possible?

Blakelaw suggests that so long as gleeon capture (or activation, if you will) occurs in sufficient proximity to other gleeon capture, these gleeons unite to share in a common field effect. A kind of resonance and this unity of effect creates a whole.

One implication is that adjacent gleeons must influence one another in some fundamental way irrespective of the level or kind of activation they enjoy, and it is not unreasonable to surmise that all sensation of any kind must therefore be supported by one single fundamental particle i.e. the gleeon, which is capable of adopting one of many possible levels of activation, along the lines found in the electron model for atoms, except that a gleeon would support single occupancy of only one valency at any time.

Thus, the lowest level of gleeon activation might supply only *one* feeling, for instance that of pain.

The next level of activation might offer *two* alternative feelings, for instance love or rage, but only allow one at a time.

A third level might offer *four* alternative feelings (or eight or whatever the progression is) and this might encompass sensations of heat, or pressure. In this way activation levels escalate through taste and smell and light and sound, and any other possible senses (animal, human or alien).

Elaboration: - *Emergence*

BLAKELAW SUGGESTS THAT an energy transition is required to bring a pre-conscious gleeon to activation at some level.

There is a school of thought that argues that consciousness is an emergent property.

Blakelaw argues that (i) emergent properties are different in their nature than is applicable here, and they are always explicable, which is how we know they are emergent, and (ii) the claim that consciousness is an emergent property is an admission of failure to explain it any other way.

Emergent properties are such as: (a) the laws of thermodynamics which are an emergent property of molecular motion on vast scales, (b) surface tension and menisci where fluids encounter gases or solids, (c) visible patterns, such as of triangles, that will emerge when cellular automata follow some specific set of rules.

In the case of (a) the laws of thermodynamics are explained mathematically and can be easily pictured as arising from the mass motion of molecules. This emergent behaviour is not a mystery, it is explained. With (b) again, our understanding of fluids, of hydrogen or other bonds whose energy needs must be satisfied at the boundary of a fluid, dictate that the observed phenomena of surface tension and menisci occur. With (c) patterns emerge, but it is our (human) judgement and faculties that detect these patterns (a curiosity for us) and the patterns serve no functional purpose. Even if they can be made to serve a mechanical end, like shepherding less-massive, but larger, components across some region, still *the mechanism is plain to see.*

Simply reverting to the claim "We do not understand X so X must be an emergent property" explains nothing, indeed attempts no explanation. But emergent properties are explained; it is only because of the explanation that we can properly say they are emergent.

Indeed when it comes to consciousness strange equivalences are claimed: we do not understand consciousness; we do not understand dark matter; therefore consciousness must be dark matter—why? Because they share the common feature of 'not being understood [yet] by humans'? How absurd! 'I do not understand economics' and 'I do not understand the singularity at the centre of a black hole' therefore economics is a black hole. (Well...)

The upshot is: simply claiming consciousness is an emergent property is ridiculous. We can only claim something to be an emergent property when we know how it is emergent[17].

Ultimately: an emergent property of a system belongs to an alternative descriptive paradigm of that system. One and the same system might be described via two (or more) different paradigms (an example being thermodynamics and kinetic theory).

If we evolved to be conscious, consciousness delivers a survival advantage. In order to deliver a survival advantage, consciousness must make a causal difference to the operation of the brain/mind complex.

If consciousness plays a causal role in the brain/mind complex, consciousness cannot be an emergent property of the brain since everything the brain does could then be accounted for in the lesser paradigm (i.e. the operation of the brain without the mind)—there would be no need for consciousness to enter the picture.

Thus, since consciousness plays a causal role, the brain and mind cannot be identical, and consciousness cannot be an emergent property of the brain.

(The same, of course, is true of machines.)

---

17 Notwithstanding the well-known philosophical counter-arguments to functionalism, which 'emergence' must be a subset of.

Step Fourteen - *Me-ness and Self-identity*

Idea:

IF CONSCIOUSNESS IS accounted for in terms of gleeons, how is it that 'I' am so important to 'Me'? Why do I value my life and care what happens to me, indeed care about anything?

Two important aspects of the question are (i) how can I account for the identity of self that is sustained over time? and (ii) how can I account for the me-ness of me (and possibly also the other-ness of others) that makes it important to me that 'I' continue over time?

My own sense of self is strong, but the system described so far, of gleeon capture etc. would have it that the whole thing that is me—body, brain and The Surface—changes from moment to moment. It is said that every atom in our body is replaced at least once every seven years. Like the Ship of Theseus, I am not the same physical entity I was seven years ago. Indeed, only my memory tells me I am the same person today that I was yesterday. Gleeon-based consciousness suggests I am a different person from moment to moment as Gleeons come and go. Why should the person of this moment care about the person of the next moment, let alone of the next day, or some years hence? Indeed where and how does any sense of self—of *me*—come from?

I cannot deny, in fact I must insist that I care what happens to the person I call *me*.

In the picture painted so far, continuity lies most simply in the smooth, graduated transitions that the brain orchestrates in The Surface from one moment to the next by anticipating how the world the brain has generated for us is going to change in that time.

On its own this is not sufficient to create a sense of self and any sense of continuity is weak because this mechanism offers no specific cohesion between elements, either in the moment or from moment to moment. *This* happens, then *That* happens, with some overlap, but so what?

Even adding Meaning(M) as we already do in The Surface does no more than add veridical bulk to the field of content/experience pairs as if, itself, an additional flavour. Meaning(M) neither unites our experience of the moment, nor can it contribute to continuity of experience because there is nothing to interpret it and observe that it persists since any such interpretation would require a *homunculus* or inner eye[18].

To some extent the brain can introduce some sense of cohesion by recognising objects in the world and offering a running commentary (internal discourse) of things and events in the world. Such talk might extend to talk of the self, of the body, and especially of the self as an agent, but it does not provide a feeling of the me-ness of me and of my desire to continue as this self. It is mere commentary and could be produced by a mechanical device, by programming[19], or whatever, without any need to rely on consciousness, nor generate consciousness, and therefore could operate independently of any experience of the me-ness of me, as a stream of words, albeit with Meaning(M). This is not sufficient to produce a sense of self. The feeling of value and self-worth and of wanting to continue as *an individual something* is missing.

(Would we claim that people and higher order animals that lack language thereby lack a sense of self? My answer would be no; a sense of self (and of the otherness of others) must lie elsewhere other than in language, although language might serve as an amplifier—for instance through personal outrage which, once expressed, might be sustained. But language is not the core thing that underpins our feelings of self and continuity.)

---

18 Meaning(M) subsists in The Surface and is not perceived in conjunction with other elements of The Surface; a conjunction would be a logical device and require an observer to appreciate it.

19 For example a software program reporting on measurements taken from the brain.

Let us extend our analysis to what memory and anticipation might bring with them.

First and foremost, we do not store feelings (pain, joy, fear etc.) in memory. Feelings can only exist in The Surface. Feelings are generated in The Surface by the brain when events are recalled or imagined and reproduced in The Surface[20].

Now, if we introduce memory and anticipation, which work not from moment to moment but on the scale of hours, days, weeks etc., then we introduce what we might refer to as a brooding element. This brooding element of body-brain-surface allows us in the Now to anticipate pleasure and pain in the future (or to remember it from the past), its being manifest through weak non-veridical feelings. Hence 'we' can come to 'want' the more intense feelings which would accompany the veridical perception that would result were the scenario we imagine realised.

Of course 'we' and 'want' still need to be explained in terms of the body-brain-surface; we must not inadvertently introduce circularity (or the *homunculus*). 'We' and 'want' are at the core of the thing we are trying to explain.

Let us refine the triad we are dealing with to be: senses-brain-surface to emphasise the role played by these components, and to refine our account to what is necessary and what is not.

The 'we'[21] is the thing we seek to identify and explain. 'We' refers to the self and implicitly to a self which has a sense of continuity. We must expunge all reference to 'we' from our explanation (from the right-hand-side of the equation as it were). As to 'want', 'want' contains within it both 'we', the thing doing the wanting, and an implicit but unidentified *desiderata*.

How can the senses-brain-surface triad mechanism be made to 'want' something?

The simplest mechanism would be to hard-wire the brain so that when a pleasant memory is laid down, the memory is laid down with a marker that should such a scenario arise again, this scenario is to be preferred over others; the

---

20 Feelings might both be represented in memory in the form of an emotion-flag (or token) and also generated by the brain in the moment, from context.

21 In the text above indicating 'I' but following conventional English usage, not a slippage in logic.

converse would be true for pain. Note that this account is irrespective of e.g. the unpleasant nature of pain. A machine could be programmed to achieve this result. The 'want' here is purely functional (teleological if you like) and without feeling.

We now have a catalogue of features that would embellish a sense of self but which do not, even when taken all together, produce that sense of self, because you can strip them all away and plausibly believe what is left (in an animal or infant) retains its sense of self, and this is not anthropomorphism since the individual so-stripped can be seen to conduct itself in the world as an individual.

Ultimately, something is missing from our account.

LET US BRIEFLY revisit the causal account of the role of consciousness.

We have evolved to be conscious because consciousness confers a survival advantage to those creatures that possess it. To offer such an advantage consciousness must play a causal role in the operation of the brain/mind. We know that consciousness follows brain activity by a small delay. So action in-the-moment and reaction in-the-moment do not rely on a contribution from consciousness; the contribution of consciousness must be on a longer timescale i.e. via the formation of memories. Memories will include markers for feelings, pleasure, pain and so on, and the brain can reproduce those feelings in The Surface when those memories are recalled.

However these markers are all laid down mechanically, so consciousness would seem not to be required if one were to create a machine that is designed to reproduce such memory-formation and thereby reproduce the conduct of a conscious entity. We need only reproduce the mechanical operation of the brain...

This is contrary to the argument from evolution which tells us that consciousness plays a causal role and makes a difference to the way a creature conducts itself in the world.

Thus the presence of consciousness must do something more than merely add strength or weakness or other emphasis to memories.

Some aspect of the intermediation of consciousness cannot be replicated by the physical mechanisms of the brain —or perhaps can only be reproduced *mechanically* with gross inefficiencies and the consequence that a conscious entity will wildly outperform an unconscious one.

We might say the coming and going of individual gleeons makes a difference, e.g. the hysteresis effect suggested by Blakelaw in MIMH[22], whereby the laying down of memories involves specific patterns of delays. But this is merely a mechanism of communication, of conveying data, a chain of cause and effect, albeit with a delay However when the mechanism involves neurons (and/or other brain cells) why can't the neurons simply add the delay themselves? The neurons must be capable of that degree of sensitivity to time since they are conveying the result to memory with that exact self-same sensitivity to time. Thus the issue is not one of causal (communicative) mechanism but of content.

If the crucial difference is not in the coming and going of gleeons then it lies in the interaction between gleeons.

We have already postulated that gleeons interact with one another, not least to align (in what we have suggested is their lowest energy state) to form a spheroidal surface, orientated towards some notional centre. Gleeons in the gleeon field must be close enough to one another to causally affect each other. This proximity in the gleeon field achieves a coherence effect among gleeons and thereby the unity of effect that we have referred to elsewhere as our internal cinema screen[23].

If the content of the field makes a difference to the way memories are laid down in the brain and the content is not a matter of individual gleeons then we need to look toward patterns of gleeons, such as localisations or concentrations of pain, or of symmetries and resonances which might contribute to, let us say, aesthetic effects.

These effects must be too costly for the brain to easily reproduce mechanically.

Blakelaw suggests that such Surface-mediated (gleeon-field) responses might fine-tune a creature's overall

---

22 Hysteresis: the value one physical variable takes on as the function of another, depends on the direction of travel of the variable. If function R is the rate of increase of X compared to Y when Y is increasing, the rate of decrease of X compared to Y is not negative-R when Y is decreasing.

23 There may be other gleeon fields and individual gleeons generated in the brain, but we are only aware of those that are able to lay down memories, and it would seem for most of we human beings there is a monopoly of one in that role.

behaviour so as neither to be too sensitive, or to over-react, or to react too swiftly to some stimulus (any of which might be characterised as 'neurotic'), nor to under-react to the stimulus (which might be characterised as 'lethargic').

One might also ask how the brain so accurately and acutely takes advantage of, and benefits from, this precisely tuned feature of a gleeon field, to which the answer must be that the brain and the nature of the gleeon-field it generates evolved together from the simplest brain-cell arrangements in the simplest creatures. Thus the two have always complemented each other exactly and only ever become more precise, efficient and effective in that arrangement—as the two developed in symbiosis it is not merely natural but inevitable that they evolve to an optimum apportionment of cause and effect i.e. to survive competitively.

RETURNING TO THE discussion of self and me-ness we can, without recourse to a *homunculus*, talk of a unified gleeon field as a field of raw experience (albeit with Meaning(M)) but existing only in the moment.

What is missing are elaborations of the notions of wanting, and caring, and valuing the self.

Let us take the essence of all these to be some kind of 'yearning' which we all of us possess as motivation to continue to exist.

Any such 'yearning' cannot be introduced in conjunction with the usual content in The Surface. I.e. if the Surface contains the representation of a banana and we know it to be a banana (Meaning(M)) we cannot allow this 'yearning' to be applied to the banana in The Surface, since that conjunction ('banana' AND 'yearning') would require we introduce a homunculus to make sense of it.

Observe, however, that Meaning(M) is not something we perceive. It is intrinsic to some particular area of the gleeon field and in this sense is unnoticed.

So too must the 'yearning' we speak of here be unnoticed. Indeed it must be so similar in this respect to Meaning(M) that we might properly label it Yearning(Y).

Yearning(Y) does not apply to those things in the gleeon field that are currently derived from the senses. Yearning(Y) is not about the Now, but rather, about what will come. It is a yearning for the future, for change—*for what comes next.*

Yearning(Y) will accompany all those things that are anticipated by the mechanism of the brain, the anticipated behaviour of everything in the world as created by the brain from data coming from the senses.

Yearning(Y) + the anticipated behaviour of objects and materials in the world is what draws each of us into the future and is the core element of the desire for the continued self.

This combination gifts us value, and continuity, and identity which, though simple and miniscule in itself, taken across the whole Surface, for every anticipated behaviour (and the brain generates anticipations for data from all senses all the time), a core aspect of each of us wants to continue.

The primary role of the gleeon field is not to give pain its nastiness, nor make a joy of pleasure, but to give the self a desire to continue. The desire to continue gives the creature its primary advantage over any machine. A machine does not *viscerally* care whether it lives or dies; a conscious creature does; a conscious creature cares that what happens next includes it—that it carries forward into *what happens next.*

FINALLY ONE MIGHT ask how could such a mechanism evolve?

In a primitive creature, perhaps consisting of no more than a single cell, we might postulate a receptor (of light or of a chemical or of pressure) and an actuator (to re-arrange components within the cell), these two providing a feedback loop, sensitive to the light or chemical or whatever, and beneficially adjusting the arrangement of components in the cell.

The cell need only develop a causal path that anticipates the result of the coming adjustment, thereby making its adjustments prior to the arrival of the stimulus, which improves its efficiency, and for that causal path to capture gleeons that will function as behavioural anticipation, and to capture gleeons that will function with Yearning(Y)—both within the same field—for the single-cell creature to have some sense of self, and value and a will to survive.

This is not to claim that this is what happens or that this single-cell creature exists anywhere; it is only to observe that *probably* the will to survive arrived in Nature before fully-fledged perception of the world, and that no great evolutionary step is required in carbon-based lifeforms to move from chemical machine to purposeful (conscious or proto-conscious) creature.

Step Fifteen - *Morality*

Idea:

DOES CONSCIOUSNESS PLAY a causal role in morality, or does consciousness merely re-present a purely mechanical moralising activity of the brain?

Our talk of moral activity is of (i) those who are capable of moral actions and moral choices (moral agents), and the degrees to which they are capable and/or are culpable (moral responsibility), and (ii) those to whom moral considerations extend (moral patients), and the degree to which such considerations extend (moral worth).

Capable and culpable are similar in scope but not necessarily aligned. In a *Sophie's Choice* scenario any choice made is made by a capable agent who is not culpable.

A man might be a moral agent, but the degree to which he is effective can be limited by his ability to reason morally as well as by his general problem-solving skills. For instance, were an ambulance driver called upon to save both a drowning child and to collect a pensioner with a broken wrist, he might choose to fetch the pensioner first and take a short cut which crashes the ambulance into a low bridge, in which case both his moral reasoning and his problem-solving skills are flawed. He is unbelievably morally inept for the first; he is an idiot for the second. To forgive him the first (i.e. not hold him morally culpable) he would probably have to be so mentally incapable as to be prohibited from driving in the first place. And yet he might unhesitatingly dive in to save the child if faced with the choice of doing so or doing nothing.

In the ambulance example the man finds himself reasoning in a social context, weighing perhaps death against pain in two different people, possibly aware of different time-frames, and presumably appreciating the different vulnerabilities of the two cases.

But at its most fundamental, to whom do we ascribe moral agency, and to what do we attribute moral worth?

Consider a solitary gorilla in a moated enclosure in a zoo. A small bird, a fledgling, falls into the moat and is going to drown. With the palm of one hand facing upward, fingers outstretched, the gorilla lifts the struggling bird from the water, places it gently on the bank and proceeds, softly, to blow on it.

Is this rescue a moral act?

Plainly yes; the gorilla has saved the bird's life for no benefit to itself.

But we do not believe the gorilla possesses spoken or written language in which to reason, nor does it belong to a social group where things such as 'picking birds out of water' is learnt behaviour. Indeed the bird is not only a different species but there is no conceivable benefit to the gorilla in saving the bird (no symbiotic foraging, nor appreciating birdsong, nor the prospect of friendship—although one might want to attribute some hope for company to the lonely gorilla; however if the gorilla knows that a bird might drown, it likely knows that birds do and will fly, and they fly *away*). The gorilla merely felt compelled to rescue the bird (it was a deliberate, skilful act, with a clear goal, successfully carried out to completion).

This suggests that any conscious creature might be a candidate for moral agency and might (separately) be worthy of moral consideration.

We think of moral acts as having visceral force while also being automatic, akin to a reflex. This imperative—this apparent feeling of necessity—accompanies our thought or goal in any moral act. Where there is feeling there is activity in The Surface. The question becomes one of whether the activity in The Surface plays a direct causal role in the moral act, or whether such feeling is generated in The Surface by the brain in order e.g. to facilitate the laying down of memories of a certain kind, with a certain special strength, for future reference[24].

---

24 Although, if the brain merely lays down memories of moral behaviour in a way to make it more likely that such (patterns of) behaviour will be repeated, what is it about those behaviours that

The gorilla example suggests that moral behaviour is not learned. It is an action taken in the moment in a unique scenario for which, as far as the moral agent is concerned, there is no alternative and it need have no antecedent. It cannot be hard-wired nor is there any previous conditioning from which this action might be generalised[25].

The mind/brain decides in the now that such-and-such action in such-and-such unique scenario surpasses all other possible actions (or inactions). Furthermore, the action must be with reference to something the gorilla understands, and appreciates (i.e. the bird, the object in the world).

If we are to attribute morality the unique quality that it is not learned behaviour and yet has its own imperative force, then we must seat it in consciousness and find its value in something other than the memory-reinforcement role that consciousness, in general, plays[26].

The only, and obvious, candidate we have for this is the self-worth of the individual—the me-ness of me—the need for the continued self.

If the need for the continued self is generalised to other creatures then they are worthy of the same (or at least similar) special consideration that we apply to ourselves i.e. above and beyond being mere bio-chemical machines.

This appreciation for other creatures is what imparts unconditional value to them for their own sake in the mind/brain of the moral agent, and is what underpins all

---

makes them morally worthy?

25 Possibly: is the gorilla copying something a zookeeper has done? Is the gorilla mirroring itself being saved from water as an infant by its mother? But in either case, what motivates the gorilla in the saved fledgling example? A purely learned reflex would have it rescue any detritus from the water, but here it recognises a living creature. The fact that it responds to a living creature means it appreciates the life of the creature. Suppose the gorilla had learned to net pondweed out of the moat and dash it, roughly, on the bank, surely it would give any creature it netted a different treatment, following the evidence of the fledgling example, above?

26 Learning belongs to the brain, as does reasoning (and reasoning takes time, while the imperative is an impulse), nor can the imperative be a reflex since a reflex requires a prior pattern—previous experience—to learn (any such reflex is in a world, if not social, context which, unlike a muscular reflex, has to be learnt post-partum).

moral reasoning and worth-giving, singly or in a wider social context[27].

The generalisation is not, however, consciously a logical or rational one. It is a simple, unconscious, unmediated, unthought-about, automatic, projection from the mind/brain of the moral agent to other objects in the world (i.e. creatures, would-be moral patients) that are considered to possess consciousness to the degree that the moral agent can form a Theory of Mind for the creature. For one creature to possess a *Theory of Mind* with regard to another creature is to say the first attributes some degree of consciousness, feelings, and thought processes to the second[28].

If the moral imperative is towards a moral patient that is either thought about (imagined) or directly present in The Surface, how is the moral imperative associated with the moral patient unless by generating 'moral feelings' in The Surface (i.e. as content/experience pairs, or *qualia*) in conjunction with the appearance (or ghost-behaviour) of the moral patient in The Surface?

The possible difficulty being (i) we cannot allow logical conjunctions in The Surface, since they would require an inner eye to make sense of them, and (ii) if the brain inserts such feelings, there is no need for consciousness to play a role, consciousness could merely re-present some construct or other from the brain, like any sound, or colour, or emotion.

However this possible difficulty does not arise because the moral imperative applies to whatever is the focus of attention at the time, which is the region in The Surface where the brain is busiest finding Meaning(M) and (presumably)anticipating behaviours (both actions and outcomes). The will to act i.e. to respond to the imperative once the object-in-the-world is given value, needs no further mediation or experience in the Surface, although other emotions may come into play (fear, joy and so on)—but these are no more than side-effects.

---

27 If the appreciation is maintained over an extended period towards a single moral patient it underpins empathy; in the absence of alternative motives it is the essence of altruism; it is not however anthropomorphism in which human-like thoughts and feelings are <u>inappropriately</u> attributed to another creature.

28 Thought processes do not require language; I do not deliver a running commentary to myself when I decide to cross a road: I merely see a gap in the traffic and navigate it.

Ultimately, by identifying the core of the moral imperative as a projection of the me-ness of the moral agent to the moral patient we have the basis of a *do-as-you-would-be-done-by* moral system which lends itself most directly to an aversion to the killing of others.

However, not all moral agents are equal in their capacity for moral reasoning.

Natural variations in the brains of the members of any species will result in different degrees of both the sense of *me-ness* and of the ability to project that *me-ness*[29]. In humans, the imperative to act on that projected *me-ness* might be culturally curtailed (i.e. selectively suppressed): apes, monkeys, cows, dogs and dolphins all receive different treatments as moral patients in different parts of the world[30]. We might accept that a fly is alive and even has some fledgling consciousness but we might also think nothing of swatting it (and of course a mosquito might present a threat to the me-ness of me and be sought out for destruction, following some system of moral reasoning). A rat, we might appreciate can feel pain and enjoy some degree of emotion (they are known to laugh), but we have an aversion to them, which is likely learned, although possibly trades on some innate feeling of disgust for creepy-crawlies in general. And for the most part we withdraw our moral attitude from them, and ignore any passing moral distaste when it comes to disposing of them (we *look the other way*, which we can now comprehend in an entirely new light).

All this is <u>not</u> to say Moral Relativism is tenable (Moral Relativism is the idea that, for instance, while in Society A it is wrong to kill, in Society B it is acceptable to kill, thus killing in Society B should be tolerated by Society A without the need to intervene because Society A 'believes in' Moral Relativism). Moral Relativism is incoherent because all moral activity derives from the same projection (or generalisation) of the *me-ness* of me; all humans possess

---

29 The Surface is a product of the brain. The brain develops from DNA in a physical environment. Brains will necessarily differ from one agent to the next; Surfaces will necessarily differ from one agent to the next. But the Surface will always have some sense of me-ness since predictive behaviour and Yearning(Y) are core functions which in evolutionary terms (explanatorily and hence most likely) pre-date full-on consciousness.

30 We might say that moral reasoning mediates, enhances, or pollutes, the essential moral imperative.

that *me-ness* and all humans project it; it is integral to the Surface and in its essence is unmediated by either rational thought or by social construct. It generalises the moral imperative without moderation and without limit[31] [32]. Any question of degree, which might result from social conditioning, is irrelevant. Morally legitimate social reasoning attempts to solve moral dilemmas (essentially moral paradoxes, i.e. where conflicting moral imperatives cannot be satisfied) with least harm; social reasoning does not and cannot specify absolute moral goods (though many a politician might wish otherwise). Killing people is wrong.

Above, we have hinted at the idea of primary and secondary virtues[33]. And, given the moral schematic described above, it is possible to group moral reasoning into certain types:

THE PRIMARY VIRTUE is that life should continue (do not kill, and always intervene to avert death). This is an unmediated imperative. It is almost as hard-wired as the will of the self to survive.

The secondary virtues apply to pain, harm, and suffering which should not be inflicted and should be averted when discovered. These imperatives are brain-mediated, which is to say they rely on the agent's Theory of Mind with regard to the patient.

---

31 Besides, tolerance is a social construct, a product of moral reasoning, a secondary virtue. Tolerance is not the principle that underpins all moral reasoning. The unmediated me-ness imperative is the ultimate and only source of morality. It would be an error of logic to use tolerance as the reason to deny the primary virtue, since no principle (i.e. of pure value) would be left to sustain such tolerance.

32 Principle X cannot have both absolute universal application AND vary from individual to individual. Moral principles and objective facts cannot be both true and contradictory. Nor can any coherent system be built on subjective opinions: if A's opinion offends B and B's opinion offends A are both to go to jail? In which case presumably the jailer offends both parties and will be forced to join them in the same cell. Besides which the mere suggestion (let alone application) of any kind of 'universal subjective law' offends this author...

33 Usage here is confined to this text and is not intended to reference any other philosophical systems, definitions, or distinctions.

The tertiary virtues also apply to pain, harm and suffering, but where such things are rationally or socially mediated, for instance, "It's only a rat," or "the ambulance crew need to move the accident victim out of the rain (who am I to judge whether or not he needs a neck-brace?)"

Societal 'virtues' are a culturally influenced calculus that ranks, compares, and judges disparate and competing tertiary virtues for the self-serving pragmatic goals of a society (i.e. moral goods or ills do not have to be the most significant considerations, indeed may not be factored in at all). For example: A prisoner might go to jail for some combination of: protecting the public (prevent further crime), offering rehabilitation, demonstrating public opprobrium, taking public revenge, and intentionally cause discomfort both to motivate the prisoner to desist in their activities, and to deter others from similar unlawful actions. Social virtues need have nothing to do with morality, although politicians will try to dress their expediency in terms of moral necessity, which of course is dishonest.

Moral paradoxes are those cases, like Sophie's Choice, or the standard philosophical problem of 'by taking one simple action and killing N people, you can save (N+1) people'. There is no correct moral solution to such a problem. Why should there be? You cannot remove the morality from the scenario, you can only do your best to weigh all the factors and outcomes that are morally and rationally available to you... but you cannot avoid this being an exercise in societal virtues and it is a fallacy to try to make it otherwise.

NOTE THAT 'SOCIETY' cannot be a moral patient. A group of people might form a legal entity, but morality comes down to individuals acting for or against individuals. Again politicians might find it convenient to group and name collections of individuals, as either patients or agents, but as can be seen from the above reasoning neither group culpability (as a collective agent) nor group merit targeting (as a collective patient) can have any moral traction.

Ultimately each individual is responsible for the actions each takes for or against one or more individuals.

As to the apparent 'feeling of necessity' mentioned at the beginning of this section: we cannot allow an additional feeling to be instantiated in the Surface. The apparent feeling of imperative merely reflects the fact that the action the agent carries out, is performed of necessity, which is an observable fact, explained in terms of interior discourse as "I had to do it!"—*sans* rationalisation. At its heart morality is not reflective; moral reasoning **is** reflective, but reasoning occurs after the fact of some kind of moral situation, or moral intuition, and after the accompanying moral imperative in that situation has arisen.

Elaboration:

IF WE HAVE successfully reduced morality to a causal feature in The Surface, i.e. a consequence of the way we are conscious, how can our morality have any moral force? i.e. in the sense of an ultimate Good or Bad. If morality is merely a 'mechanical' cause and effect thing, it happens because, well, that sort of thing would happen wouldn't it? You would feel inclined that way, wouldn't you? You would naturally be so-motivated, etc. Where then is any moral imperative that one *should* do one thing rather than another? It would seem that, in fact, any moral action, any moral choice, merely follows an impulse that arises from a series of pretty much arbitrary events in the universe, i.e. the interplay of sub-atomic particles in the brain.

Besides if it can be fully explained (and surely there must be some explanation), whatever that explanation may be, we will have explained morality away and robbed it, in some sense, of its value.

Put another way, there is no deity laying down absolute values of Good or Bad. It's kind of 'up to you'. Value, such as it is, lies only in the natural urge for conscious life to continue. Why should that have any value at all, other than be 'nice' for the consciousness involved? Morality needs something more, surely? It needs a universal rule that says something like: Consciousness is the most valuable commodity in the universe and it is morally wrong to knowingly destroy it. Even then, we are smuggling in 'morally wrong' without explanation or justification.

It seems that if we can explain morality in terms that do not render it *sui generis*, we have explained it away, and robbed it of value.

But perhaps this is a matter of levels of description, and how we describe a mechanism and its effects. Morality, in the end, is the imperative—not the mechanism that brings it about, nor the context in which it arises. It is the 'feeling of necessity' sans rationalisation and, counter-intuitively (as explained in this section) without feeling in any normal (Surface, content/experience pair) sense.

A MORAL IMPERATIVE does not come from God or the Universe, so where does it get its value from? Why is it not merely another fact about the world? But there is intrinsic value or intrinsic worth in any moral imperative since it comes from an essential aspect of each of us. Each of us (all of us) must (in the strongest sense) value our own lives and seek to survive; this is not a conscious thought, nor a rationalisation; it is inbuilt into consciousness.

Step Sixteen - *Aesthetics*

Idea:

IT IS OBVIOUS that consciousness is a necessary component in our appreciation of works of art, whether the art is a rousing orchestral piece, a poignant portrait on canvas, a novel of just deserts, or a romantic movie—we have not only an emotional response but there is some sense in which we can say all these works of art, across various mediums, are beautiful.

In the above examples we capture two key features of effective art: the artist has stirred our emotions while also touching our aesthetic sensibility.

To the extent that emotions are stirred, we already have an account of the brain recalling memories and generating the associated emotions for those memories. The scheme is easily adapted to the images, sounds, words, vicarious experience, and so on fed us by the artist. This part of an explanation seems sufficient: emotions are induced by an effective narrative (understood in a very broad sense) and mediated by the brain.

The other aspect, that of beauty, which adds an extra piquancy to the emotional experience, is harder to pin down.

Undoubtedly beauty is to be found in nature: a beautiful landscape, a handsome horse, a sunflower in full bloom. The artist's job involves capturing the essence of it and passing that essence on to us (or inventing something equally as effective in this regard). But this essence is not like emotions or other feelings. We neither feel it 'in our gut' (as one might with love or rage), nor as a *component* of some object represented in The Surface (as one might a colour, or a sound), and yet, like the moral imperative, the aesthetic response is associated with what the brain is focused on, and busy establishing Meaning(M) for, in the moment (a work of art, for example a framed painting on a wall, will most likely occupy only one small portion of the field of view, and that is where the brain will be focussing its attention during the aesthetic episode).

The question is: are the known, analytical and technical aspects of a beautiful work[34] processed solely by the brain which then triggers an aesthetic response in The Surface, or does The Surface play a causal role in the production of an aesthetic response? That is: does some kind of resonant effect in the gleeon field contribute to our special sense of satisfaction and completeness and joy in the work of art?

We are looking for a single phenomenon that delivers an aesthetic response to a wide range of artistic endeavours: from a sculpture which is a three-dimensional tactile and visual piece, to music which might be a one-dimensional stream of tones[35], or we might have a combination of artistic mediums, such as a beautiful movie.

It is easy to say that a movie might be frame-by-frame beautiful. But the story, too, might be beautiful. As with music, the component parts of the story are distributed over time (although you might insist that a beautiful story can only be judged as beautiful—or not—at its end).

How can music be beautiful? Certainly there is an element of anticipation, exercising the 'anticipatory behaviour' aspect of The Surface. Perhaps there is aesthetic satisfaction when actual data confirms anticipated data? But no: that cannot be a candidate for the aesthetic response since that is happening all the time across most, if not all, of the Surface (Step 7).

Is our only option to revisit the question of how can an aesthetic response be provided by the brain? For instance, the brain might generate 'beauty *qualia*' alongside and interspersed among other *qualia* (content/experience pairs)

---

34 The golden ratio, a tried-and-tested colour palette, the impact of the work in the context in which it is presented and so on.

35 It might be stereo and the brain might render different tones from different three-dimensional locations in an orchestra pit, but at the extreme it can be a simple tonal sequence from a single point in space and still be beautiful.

in The Surface, i.e. those qualia that correspond to the beautiful thing. Except we run into the problem of conjunction: we cannot have the content/experience pairs for a painting adjacent to the content/experience pairs of aesthetic appreciation since that would require an inner eye to make sense of the combination i.e. to recognise and make sense of the conjunction[36]. Possibly an aesthetic response could be a feeling in the gut, like love and rage, but surely our experience of the aesthetic is *in the thing itself.*

Suppose then, that the would-be aesthetic object or sequence triggers some kind of resonance response in The Surface, how would that manifest causally in the brain (i.e. so the Surface is making a difference), and what would it do to our experience—how would we know one way or another? Indeed, how *do we* encounter the beauty of the thing?

Is it merely that we are drawn to the art object? Fascinated by it. When this resonance occurs the brain is caused to linger, and is caused to sustain whatever emotion has been induced by the object or sequence[37].

A machine might learn many artistic rules of thumb but can never validate anything it produces by running it through a conscious mind. It can neither know when it produces Art nor recognise Art when Art is presented to it (above and beyond the few rules of thumb that belong to any craft).

So, what makes a thing beautiful? Resonance in the gleeon field.

What does an aesthetic response amount to? That we cannot help ourselves but linger over the art object,

---

36 We might want to say that a gleeon can attain a super-state which is the aesthetic state, like the spin on a fundamental particle in physics, so the gleeon bears both a visual experience and the aesthetic response to the visual experience, which is all controlled by the brain. However to do so individually for all the gleeons of an artistic object does not explain the unity of effect in the art object and would seem only to disguise the problem of conjunction.

37 The causal connection postulated for gleeon-to-brain is via gleeon decay over time. Gleeons may decay more slowly when the gleeon field resonates locally as a result of its bearing the representation of a work of art. Further, resonance is also possible in time-based pieces since a resonant waveform might be set up between the currently veridical gleeons and the gleeons which, in lesser numbers, represent anticipated behaviours—the next phrase of music to come.

fascinated by the experience of it, with the additional (motivating and pleasurable) benefit of sustaining any emotional response we have to it.

Can this be mechanically reproduced by the brain? No, emotion is only available in The Surface, as also is an 'appreciation' of the lingering, i.e. of time (See later paper in this text re: time).

Step Seventeen - *A Standard Model*

Idea:

WE HAVE INTRODUCED the gleeon as the smallest and only essential component of consciousness, as being capable of excitational states that create various content/experience pairs.

We have described it with the simplest possible life cycle capable of accounting for all the phenomena it gives rise to: a pre-conscious gleeon is captured by the brain in a manner that activates a sensation; the gleeon decays sometime later, releasing the energy of capture back to the brain, and the delay and rate of decay provide a causal mechanism by which the gleeon influences the laying down of memories.

We have borrowed from the current best picture of the smallest scale of physics, which is to say the Standard Model of particles, which is understood in terms of (probabilistic) wave-like disturbances in quantum fields, allowing that pre-conscious gleeons appear and disappear randomly as noise throughout the universe; they may be captured by a suitable mechanism that activates them as a content/experience pair (as found in the brain) and using the analogy of electron shells around an atom (<u>and no more than an analogy</u>)[38], we postulate different 'shell' levels (corresponding to different senses and the range of sensations that belong to those

---

38 It can only be a rough analogy because in atoms electrons fill all the states they can, given the number and energy of available electrons, whereas for a gleeon, we envisage one state only being occupied for any one gleeon.

senses) and different numbered states, as it were, within the shells, representing specific sensations within each range.

We introduced gleeons of Meaning(M) and Yearning(Y), but during the course of our analysis we found we are forced to rule out the possibility of what we called gleeon *conjunctions* in The Surface. If we require that some gleeon X be associated with some other gleeon Y in order to provide an explanation of some phenomenon or other, we have inadvertently re-introduced the Inner Eye, or *homunculus*, because any such conjunction (sensation P AND sensation Q) requires interpretation. Interpretation of any kind is what we are trying to explain and part of that explanation requires a purely *felt* Surface.

However we can borrow from physics to accommodate Meaning(M) and Yearning(Y) if these specify a simple additional property for any gleeon. If we do this, we do however need a third state, which is one of raw or simple, unmediated sensation (for a shape in the dark that we do not recognise, or the sound of a language we do not know). This we can call Raw(R).

We now characterise a gleeon as being either pre-conscious or conscious (conscious here meaning that it produces a single content/experience pair).

If conscious, then it has state, a level, and level-content.

The state is one of Yearning(Y), Raw(R), or Meaning(M).

Levels and level-content can be tabulated, as shown for the major sense organs (below), and a conscious gleeon can only have one active level, and within that level only one active level-content:

level	level-content	sense organ
pain	pain	any part of the body
emotion	love rage fear hope etc.	musculature, especially viscera
visual	colours of the rainbow	eyes
audio	fine-grained between low and high pitch	ears
smell	fine-grained	nose
taste	sweet, sour, bitter, salt	tongue

Figure 1: Towards a Standard Model for gleeons

How brain cells capture gleeons is unknown. Specific three-dimensional patterns of charged fields, produced by chemical activity in microstructures in brain cells (most probably the neurons) might be all that is required. A physical analogy would be using a steel spanner to shape and guide a blob of impact putty (impact putty being normally soft and malleable to gradual changes, but becoming hard and resilient if anything hits it; embed the spanner slowly then yank it hard, and the putty resiliently adopts the shape and turns with the spanner, before gradually softening once pressure is off). The steel spanner would be the cell structure. The soft putty, the pre-conscious gleeon; the hard putty, the activated gleeon.

Step Eighteen - *Experimental Validation*

Idea:

HOW MIGHT ONE establish that a mechanism in the brain such as the one described here exists and is a viable candidate for delivering conscious experience?

Not only is consciousness not objectively measurable (or observable), and experiments to create consciousness artificially would be unethical, as would bombarding a living brain in a particle accelerator (if that were even possible), but also this logical analysis can only point to a *mechanism-in-principle* without specifying which physical forces are involved, or how, except to indicate scale and location (i.e. cells in the brain).

Is the gleeon not just a particle that is defined by all the mysterious work we have decided it must do and thereby more a statement of the problem than a description of the mechanism of the solution? Is this not a theory that can be neither proved nor disproved and therefore belongs to the realms of pseudo-science?

The answer to these concerns must be that the experimental journey to the heart of consciousness is not made in one step; there is no single all-revealing test, or apparatus, experiment or scenario which would support the theory in all its detail. Aspects of the theory need to give rise to hypotheses that are capable of experimental disproof. But it is impossible to prove that a non-existent thing does not exist, for instance if you doubt the existence of gleeons, which places a philosophical analysis such as this at a disadvantage.

The experimental investigation into how we achieve consciousness must be one of chipping away at component aspects, examining the brain to understand flows of data, and correlations with a wide range of reported experience, some natural, some artificially stimulated.

The question will be answered by 'learning the territory' of the brain in its minutiae and following the arrows (as it were) that say 'this way lies consciousness.' There will not be one experiment, but many. A paradigm of the functioning, conscious brain will be constructed, and become ever more refined, until it can be said "It is this operation that yields consciousness, there is no smaller component part we can go to, and indeed it is or is not *obviously* part of a Surface which, if so, is something we have some chance of understanding because of the gleeon/Surface theory."

This may or may not prove to be the case.

Alternatively, while pursuing this investigative route, some other new and greater insight, perhaps new models for thinking, or a new mathematical calculus will come along, or a deeper understanding of the Standard Model which encompasses consciousness *of necessity*, in which case, perhaps, the best that can be hoped for gleeon/Surface research is to say: "It was a necessary step along the way and a useful driver for valuable research, some usefully productive and some usefully unproductive."

Ultimately though, the gleeon/Surface model does offer a viable solution if one accepts that subjective experience is a fundamental property of the universe and it has no inherent structure (i.e. it is not a *homunculus*).

The theory is open to two avenues of experimental investigation: the essential nature of sensation and how the homunculus is defeated.

At the lowest level experimentation should in the first place be looking for the latent absorption and release of energy in e.g. neurons, i.e. where energy seems to disappear for some (short) time in conjunction with apparent sensation/experience. Such experimentation could be extended to show (or not) that latent energy absorption in one neuron can affect latent energy absorption in a nearby neuron, thereby suggesting a field effect between them that is otherwise unobserved, but might arise only at certain levels of neuronal stimulation e.g. those that might correspond to the presentation of an artistic work.

The homunculus is defeated via the Surface which, while having not being fixed spatially and so not observable under the microscope, is subject to psychometric testing, such as the degree of understanding needed by an individual for peripheral objects to be accepted without question, as in dreams.

Step Nineteen - *The Good Society*

Idea:

HAVING USED THE gleeon/Surface model of consciousness to define morality, can we (should we?) extrapolate beyond the individual and ask how a good and fair society might be constituted?

Elaboration:

A GOOD SOCIETY allows all individuals to act well while moderating conflicts of interest (both moral and civic) proportionately and without favour, thereby making it also a fair society.

Moral Relativism is untenable and a good society must prohibit some core transgressive acts, regardless the cultural history or norms of those who belong to the society.

While a good society seeks to be tolerant, to advocate freedom over slavery (whether slavery is to an individual, to a corporation, to a dogma, or to society itself), it cannot tolerate actions that would undermine itself as an otherwise tolerant society.

A good society is one in which all voices are allowed to be heard, all interests taken into consideration, moral conflicts and moral paradoxes are avoided where possible, but when encountered are dealt with openly and fairly.

Given human foibles, weakness, greed, error and so on, such a society might never be achieved, but a society that seeks to achieve such an elusive goal will serve its citizens better than one which makes no effort to escape corruption and mediocrity, conceals error, and which rules by fear or favour, brutality or dogma, or favours manipulation and propaganda over informed, open debate.

A good society must necessarily be open. There can be no hidden societal agendas, and all actions and decisions taken in the public interest must be open to public scrutiny.

These *desiderata* are perhaps obvious and uncontroversial. Who would not want to live in such a society? Indeed, one would have to question the motives of anyone who disagreed with such desiderata, but still: what role does morality play (in particular morality rooted in the gleeon/Surface) because surely also, one could conceive of a society that might claim to meet such *desiderata* but which turned out to be a mean-spirited hell[39].

Elaboration:

WHILE A GOOD society might embrace any number of cultures, the society itself needs a meta-culture which corresponds to, implements, and is encapsulated in its *social reasoning*.

This has its corollary in the Laws of Nature, especially the laws of physics, that result in the universe functioning consistently and uniformly and which reliably deliver the mechanism whereby consciousness, and thereby morality, come about.

The meta-culture is the framework of laws, rules, regulations and infrastructure that supports openness and fairness. It is the engine of social reasoning.

In particular, for the framework to be robust and effective and to last over time, power cannot reside in one place, nor in a single hierarchy.

Monolithic systems fail. They become corrupt (if not corrupt to begin with) because there can be no unassailable checks and balances inside the monolith. At any level of the

---

39 Beggar-thy-neighbour, accuse-thy-neighbour, a bureaucrat's fiefdom, or the petty official's wet dream, and more... any such might be made to fit the same framework as our desiderata. I.e. with regard to our definition. Yet to say in response to our desiderata: 'I know what you mean,' is wholly inadequate. There needs to be a mechanism that minimises the chances of a 'good society' emerging as some kind of a hell.

hierarchy an individual might behave badly, make mistakes, or simply not do their job, and they have only to persuade, by whatever expediency, those they report to to look the other way and the contagion persists. If one contagion can arise, others will too. Once two or more encounter each other, there will be cumulative growth. This is a ratchet effect. It can only ever go one way—the corrupted do not willingly cease their corruption.

Unchecked from beyond the bounds of the monolith, corruption can only grow. Those who embrace corruption benefit; those who do not suffer. The circle is vicious. In time, simply in order to function, the monolithic culture must be geared to reward the wrong-doer and punish the right-doer. A monolith, and the whole of society, if it operates as a monolith, will become immoral and unfair.

Any holding to account must and can only come from outside the monolith and from some agent who is equally as powerful but alternatively motivated.

And who, in the age-old question, will watch the watchmen?

The answer is to have three (or more, but three will do) entirely independent but equally powerful loci of power: A, B, and C. A audits B. B audits C. C audits A. Each might be their own monolith (including one might hope, with their own internal checks and balances), but all are open to independent scrutiny and can be brought to justice[40] [41].

---

40 One might ask: who or what is to stop the heads of A, B, and C coming to some secret arrangement? For which perhaps only pragmatic measures are possible: prohibiting the heads from ever meeting, once appointed; limiting the duration of appointment; no rotating doors; insisting that those likely to be appointed should all have their lives more than usually open to public scrutiny until appointed or not, and until any such appointment ceases; ensuring there is an effective and safe whistle-blowers' charter, because the chances are that someone, somewhere will know of any subterfuge. Furthermore some appointments must be by popular vote and open to any candidate from the general public who puts themself forward, so that bad actors, though they be supported by their own monoliths, and possibly in implicit collusion with other monoliths, or other disproportionately influential interests, can be removed if they are discovered promoting public harms.

41 If we name our types of monoliths Primary, Scrutiny, and Audit, and we have three categories of monolith: Legislators, Enforcers, and Judiciary, note that they do not necessitate duplication of function in enormous bureaucracies. Scrutiny might

Monolith

Monolith with elected positions

→ Direction of scrutiny

Primary   Scrutiny   Audit

Legislators

Enforcement

Judiciary

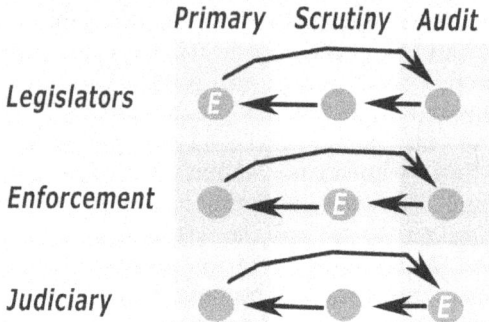

Figure 2: Circles of scrutiny among independent monoliths that have equal authority.

The point being: a good society cannot be monolithic. Also, any system will not be perfect; one can only hope to keep it pointing in the right direction, with self-correcting measures that prove adequate and harness the ingenuity of the human being to a good end, rewarding that end, making it more attractive to behave well than behave badly.

Elaboration: - *Social Reasoning*

A GOOD SOCIETY, capable of giving succour to all cultures, cannot be prescriptive in advance about the rules it creates and administers, nor in times of technological change, about the laws it deems fit in the face of technology yet to come.

What then should be the shape of the social reasoning implemented by the laws, rules, regulations and

---

need one hundredth the personnel of Primary, and Audit one hundredth the personnel of Scrutiny. Also, as envisaged (and shown in the diagram), each type will include an elected element, but the elected elements will be different for each category. The electorate has its say, but no majority can ever overthrow the system of fairness to all.

infrastructure (the meta-culture that protects and preserves all other cultures)?

Let us answer the question via a thought experiment.

Suppose a virus causes a global pandemic that infects 90% of the population of the planet, and the effect of this virus is to extend the senses in those who are exposed to it. The extended sense operates at cell level and gives rise to an entirely new and different perceptual experience which the brain can attribute to any region of the body.

Let us call the new perception *corro*, and let's say the experience of corro is manifested in one of five ways: *gam*, *gem*, *gim*, *gom*, and *gum*. It might be a little like feeling heat or cold in the body except there are five distinct and mutually exclusive 'feeling' states.

Suppose, initially, these new experiences are painless and unobtrusive and come and go at random. A mere curiosity. They do not help or hinder our lives in any way, nor do they have any knock-on side-effects.

There would be no need to legislate for or against anything relating to corro.

But suppose instead that corro was obtrusive. When anyone with corro was close to anyone else with corro, they would get a feeling of gam, gem, gim, gom, or gum. Further, let us say 'gam' is unpleasant, 'gim' is neutral and 'gum' is a delight, and the two individuals would not necessarily experience the same corro. Indeed sometimes an intense corro becomes chronically fixed.

At what point, how uncomfortable or distracting must corro be before it must be covered by legislation? It might count as a nuisance to be avoided (like a bad smell), or as real distraction (like a narcotic), or as the equivalent of physical assault.

If it sufficiently impacts everyday living and if benign conventions do not emerge that allow it to be dealt with socially and with a light touch, then legislation will be called for.

We might want to say: gam is bad; gum is good. And gam, when not an accident, should be punished.

But hard and fast rules will not be fair.

The price of a saved life might be gam (Freddie stops Frankie falling under a train after which Frankie is gam-only for all encounters and proves unable to support his family) and gum might be addictive (Juliet must fiddle the accounts else Carlos will deprive her of her gum fix and her employer goes bankrupt).

It is clear that social reasoning must reach more broadly than the immediate harms and actions or motivations of those involved.

Social reasoning must consider both the now and the future, not only for all those affected but for society as a whole—although 'making an example of someone' is patently not fair and fails the proportionality test, and attributing all ills to an unfortunate upbringing risks excusing purely malicious acts.

Ultimately corro will not and cannot be the only consideration. Social reasoning will end up weighing corro against other moral and civic values and it is not fair to restrict judgment to a single factor taken out of context. If social reasoning is not limited to a single factor then any party in any dispute must be allowed to introduce any factors they consider relevant, i.e. to be part of the reasoning process.

Which is to say that social reasoning is a multi-dimensional task. Any laws, if they express a simple societal judgment, must allow ultimate flexibility in their execution. To judge (on some occasion) whether some activity should be advocated, tolerated, or barred (succeeds or fails the test of being socially acceptable) requires looking along all these dimensions and weighing disparate factors (with futures unknown, and individual experience self-reported[42]) against each other.

One cannot legislate for all circumstances (though many a politician might claim otherwise). Social reasoning is a skill to be learned, not a calculus to be crunched.

Furthermore, simple-minded adjudication commits the Net Hook Fallacy (paper reprinted later in this text).

Controversial issues such as abortion, torture to obtain military secrets, corporal punishment, fox hunting and the paying of a ransom for hostage release, run the gamut of moral paradox to pragmatic civic choice. Social reasoning must find a way through these things without mistakenly elevating any one such complex question to a single pivotal issue and essentially equating it to a primary moral good (or bad). A paradox must be accepted as a paradox and dealt

---

42 Which is not to say unreliable but it is variable in ways which we cannot know because it relies on subjective experience.

with as best one can. Social reasoning should not moralise or find short-cuts, but should do the difficult thing, of being fair to those concerned, weighing all the factors.

Let us not forget that learning—to be disabused of naïve beliefs—is painful. Yet that fact should not stop all learning. Failure is painful, but how is anything new ever discovered unless one tries and tries and is prepared to fail? Bravery is broadly thought a good thing: to knowingly face a real and present danger in the attempt to achieve a good.

Dysfunctional social reasoning, taking easy 'moralising options', decrying all pain or discomfort as intolerably bad, would rob us of learning, of advancing, and of defending ourselves against those who would do us harm because, as has often been said: all that is required for evil to prevail is for good men to do nothing. 'Do nothing' had better not be the recommended or expeditious edict of a society. 'Doing something' usually involves change and change is uncomfortable but necessary for survival[43].

Nor should we expect a perfect world, merely one where balance, proportionality and compromise are built-in and aspired to.

Equality might be of outcomes or it might be of opportunities but it cannot be both because brains (and minds) vary in capability, capacity and learned skills.

If equality of outcomes is insisted upon then incompetent and dishonest people will be placed in positions which they are not capable of performing and will cause harms to others, in addition to which it would not be fair on those who could do the job properly but were denied the opportunity.

Whereas if equality of opportunity is insisted upon then those best able to perform functions and roles will be placed in those roles and at least society has the opportunity of operating well, and those subject to the actions of people in such roles will have the best chance of the fairest, optimum outcomes.

Wherever inequality of opportunity needs rectifying, the solution lies not in discriminating against prima facie good candidates but in implementing tests that fully and correctly

---

43 Arguably the earth's ecosystem is not, never has, nor ever can be a static system, it must continually evolve. Aspic-ation is a misguided goal.

identify aptitude and/or skill (use better tests rather than modify existing tests with additional levels of bias).

Positive discrimination is a moral hazard since real problems in the community, real fundamental discrimination and disadvantage are never corrected, always tolerated and excused, and there will forever be substandard operatives in key roles, self-sustaining mediocrity at best, and self-sustaining failure at worst, ultimately extinguishing some lives and ruining others.

A moral hazard is a real-world incentive to do the wrong thing. If there is an incentive to do the wrong thing, the wrong thing will be done.

Social reasoning is implemented and achieved on top of any rule-, regulation- or law-based mechanics through culture and convention and through the intervention of judges, magistrates and jurors who are part of that culture and able to make the complex human-centric decisions that take into account all factors that impinge upon any situation. The Intellectual Fallacy (a later chapter) tells us that it is an error to rely on rules alone. Here, one must have human intervention that relies on human judgement; formal (in this case, *legal*) models break down on first contact with reality. And there is no reasoning (and no possibility for fairness or justice) when, for example, outcomes are specified in advance.

The Nature of Evil

DOES EVIL EXIST?

At one extreme one might say that, "No—what we call 'evil' is merely a psychological state arrived at by the electrochemical constitution of the brain, in conjunction with genetics and the environment, and judged within some or other societal framework."

Or at another extreme one might say, "Yes—'evil' is a thing, an entity, an agency, a force in the universe that promotes pain and suffering, promotes bad actors and bad actions, and obstructs good actors and good actions. It is universal in its reach and universal in how we understand its effects."

Neither approach (if you forgive the cartoon characterisation) offers a particularly satisfactory picture. If Evil is merely psychological, it is merely learnt behaviour. For instance a fetish or other psychological need, perhaps to see others suffer, might be servant to a few simple psychological rewards, for instance relieving anxiety and projecting pain, to distract the sufferer from their own pain and anxiety. What is so Bad about it?—it is simply bad and pitiable.

If Evil is a force of Nature, are we to take it as having cognitive powers—the devil, if you will. What apparatus exists to create and deliver content to this devilish brain? What mechanism is employed to give the devil his universal reach?

However there are instances where (especially as one gets older) it seems there is a force of Evil: a something that can capture and consume an individual and is self-perpetuating. A something which simple psychology does not somehow capture the intensity and fervour of.

IN THE GLEEON Surface we might be able to give an account of this position of 'more than psychological imperative and less than an evil superbeing'.

We have suggested that morality is based around a *do-as-you-would-be-done-by* principle that arises from the anticipated next thing to happen, i.e. the sense of continuity that gives us our ongoing identity, our continuously unrolling anticipated (and for the most part satisfied) sensory future.

Any two-way causal interaction between the Surface and psychologically malign states would be a candidate for a universal Evil that is neither a horned creature, nor a psychotic individual.

For this account to work, ill-willed actions must in some way resonate (and serve) not just the psychology of the individual but must produce an effect in the Surface that subsequently causes reinforced and repeated behaviour of the same kind in the individual.

It would be as though the bad deeds were either sustained as an aesthetic, or as an inversion or denial of the *do-as-you-would-be-done-by* anticipatory mechanism—or a neatly resonant combination of the two.

Of course, bad deeds cannot be a simple reversal of aesthetics; Evil does not equate to bad art.

Furthermore how can an inversion of the *do-as-you-would-be-done-by* anticipatory mechanism, come about? (e.g. would we have to deprive it of its generality, or deprive it of any expected change in time, becoming less anticipatory? It is not obviously an invert-able concept. What could inversion of such a concept actually mean?).

To invert the moral imperative by behaving badly toward a moral patient (step 15) is to act in a way that is not conducive to good. It does not point to an ultimate Evil. It may simply be dull-witted self-interest.

However it does point to one possible candidate for Evil.

Evil could be said to have its roots wherever the moral imperative is not projected onto the moral patient with the same force as the moral agent applies that imperative to themselves. In the agent's felt experience moral consideration for themselves exceeds that for anyone else (or for some victim group).

(Pragmatically and emotionally you might say your close family is more important to you than anyone else in the world, but that does not deny those other people their moral worth—you merely pragmatically prioritise your attention, actions, energy etc. towards those closest to you—and quite likely those who you are most able to do something for).

Evil arises when those other individuals are denied moral worth as a matter of Surface-based fact.

Indeed Evil can come out of both an excess and absence of the *do-as-you-would-be-done-by* projection. Excess promotes Evil by the agent; Absence promotes Evil against the agent (since it renders the rest of the world as potential evil-doers, although they, by their own merits, can for the most part be expected to conduct themselves well and not succumb to this opportunity. Nonetheless the excessively fawning persona at least attracts Evil and thereby invites and promotes Evil).

The upshot is that Evil exists in the world where a Surface is not properly constituted by the brain that supports its content and reacts to its states. Evil is a global possibility, and it will follow a pattern, because the underlying mechanism is shared by all moral-capable creatures.

An Evolutionary Path to Consciousness & Two Fallacies

ONE CAN ASK: "If consciousness offers an evolutionary advantage, what was the first living thing to benefit from that advantage?" (and how did the change that introduced the advantage come about?)

Without having pinned down the precise mechanism of content/experience pair generation (or a general mechanism capable of any number of particular implementations) we cannot point to some number of living things and say such-and-such can do consciousness whereas such-and-such other cannot.

I submit that consciousness in some fashion e.g. as a simple individual content/experience pair might be present in the simplest and most primitive single-celled creatures.

That is not to claim they have 'thoughts' in any linguistic or strongly world-representing way. Merely that one or more 'sensations' occur in such creatures that would not otherwise occur in the universe were they not 'alive' i.e. functioning biologically to sustain themselves and capture and shape Gleeons.

For instance, suppose our single cell creature includes a free-floating structure of protein-like compounds that is sensitive to light, and upon being exposed to light, changes its shape, such that the single cell creature also changes shape, or rearranges its other internal structures. Perhaps doing so promotes the uptake of nutrients, or promotes a vital chemical process facilitated by light.

This most probably has a survival advantage (otherwise why is it present at all?).

It is part of a simple feedback mechanism. Here is light, adjust the cell to maximally benefit from it, or from knowing the direction it comes from.

Suppose however that when light impinges on the protein it rarely does so in a single all-covering burst. More usually light encroaches from one side or another and the protein changes configuration (relatively) gradually—or at least not all at one time. A purpose would be served by picking up the earliest change and anticipating the way the change will likely go. This too forms a feedback mechanism. What is missing, however, is a reward for correctly identifying which feedback outcomes are most beneficial.

What would constitute a reward?

It might be a simple mechanical 'I've got food' reward.

A superior version of the single cell (superior in that it improves its survival chances) will have a 'felt' feedback mechanism, wherein the piquancy of experience adds extra incentive to the single cell (taken as a whole) to adapt swiftly and efficiently to the changed lighting conditions.

It does not seem implausible to suppose that basic consciousness like this might exist in all animal forms, large and small, and possibly in vegetation too, although of course none of it will have anything remotely like our experience of the world.

The Natural-Unnatural Equivalence Fallacy

IT IS OFTEN said that because we have selectively bred animals and plants from the earliest days of humankind, that genetic modification is no different and no less safe.

This argument is false.

Evolution in Nature, and selective breeding, both require that any change is not only gradual (often from already-existing features) but also that at least one generation—and probably many—must survive and procreate and find a place in the wider environment while continuing to express whatever genetic change has come about. Only changes that pass this test (The Belongs-to-Nature test), by definition, survive in the wider world.

By contrast, genetic engineering seeks to arbitrarily introduce genes and changes to genes that have been rationally identified as 'desirable' or 'useful'. They are not put to the survive-a-generation test. Nor to the finding-a-place-in-the-environment test. Often several changes (modifications) are introduced at a time, thereby skipping several generation-survivorship tests. The changes often have nothing whatsoever to do with the base/original species, and the full consequences are not thought through because they cannot be thought through since Nature is chaotic and will always trump rationality.

The argument "There's no difference between.../Mankind has been doing it for millennia..." is a fallacy and evidence of the presence of Evil (see the chapter on Evil). Which is to say moral consideration for others is systematically ignored. For which reason all such genetic work should be de facto banned, and alternative solutions sought to the problems that the genetic techniques seek to address. For example genetic modifications could be required to be implemented one small change at a time, and to pass the 'generational survival test' with respect to the species being altered, i.e. that they can successfully procreate, and humans treated genetically or exposed to genetically modified products also need to show survival, one change at a time (inevitably slowing down progress, but avoiding a catastrophic species-ending collapse).

Genetic engineering is not the only culprit, of course. Climate engineering is another example.

The Intellectual Fallacy

THE NATURAL-UNNATURAL Equivalence Fallacy is a variant of the Intellectual Fallacy whereby the intellectual, or those who live/determine their lives largely by abstract thought, construct models of the world and make life choices, political decisions etc. by reference to these abstract world models.

The trouble is that the world is not a model and in fact is too complex to be fully modelled (chaos theory etc.) but the intellectual in question, on finding the model does not match the world, instead of rejecting or modifying the model, tries to change the world. They are too invested in their world model, or too inflexible to adapt (they tend to be intellectuals because those who are good at manipulating symbolic models are exactly those who are good at exams; this being the opposite of learning and practising skills, which are harder to judge, not least because judging a skill is itself a skill and not a tick-box exercise).

Such intellectuals prioritise the model over reality; this is what happens in those who believe they can make rational changes to natural processes and expect the Natural process to simply, predictably, and obediently comply with their wishes, as expressed in the model.

Put another way: When has the economic model of a national economy ever worked?

Time is The Ghost of the Next Thing That Might Happen

WHO DOES NOT recognise the face of a traditional clock—a flat disc with an hour hand, a minute hand, and perhaps a second hand relentlessly sweeping the clock-face alluding to some time or other via inscriptions on the perimeter?

And yet what is the stuff that makes up each perceived moment of the sweep of the hand?

As the second hand glides (or falteringly ticks) its way around the clock-face, how much of each moment of that time is ours to experience? How long does the experience of each moment linger before it is gone, forever passed?

Indeed, is our experience of each moment infinitesimally small, or is it dragged out for some extended period of time? Because, if infinitesimally small how do we perceive it at all? If dragged out, why do we not experience time in fits and starts, like a jumpy movie on a low bandwidth connection?

I'm going to offer you an answer to this question, in a roundabout way, that touches on the essence of what consciousness is by first looking at how the content of our consciousness arises.

Now, I'm not thinking of content in terms of our being aware of the blue sky because light of particular wavelengths is incident on the back of the eye, which sends signals to the brain, where they are simply converted into our personal experience of the colour blue. Instead, I want to pull that story apart a little and reconstruct it, with a twist.

When I was a student studying for a degree in physics I attended a lecture on signals and noise. That is to say we were learning about how to find good, reliable data in a signal that contained a lot of extraneous data that was pretty much random (and thereby unpredictable). If you point a telescope at the sky, you don't merely get the light from the star you are looking for; you collect light from all sorts of other sources—from dust between you and the star and so on —and this dirty, 'noisy' light corrupts what otherwise you might hope would be a pure, clear image.

In the lecture, the lecturer made his point about noise by displaying an image of the Roman numeral II on the lecture-room screen (black letters on a white background). He asked us to raise our hands if we could clearly see the numeral and everyone did so. Gradually he introduced noise into the image by way of pinpricks of dark and light across the screen until the Roman numeral disappeared behind a fine gray mist. Since he had instructed us to lower our hands once we could no longer make out the numeral II, dutifully across the lecture theatre, singly, then in pairs, and then in great swathes, student hands were lowered until not a single student claimed to see anything through the mist.

The lecturer announced that he would reverse the process and we were to raise our hands as soon as we saw the numeral II return.

The mist started to lift, vague verticals became indistinctly visible and hands were raised. However, all too soon it became apparent that we were no longer looking at the numeral II but now were presented with the numeral III and those of us who had raised our hands had done so prematurely, believing we knew already what we were going to see and, instead of seeing what was there, conjured up a II.

Of the several lessons that might be drawn from the demonstration, the loudest take-home lesson for me was that our brains create what we expect to see and they attempt to match that creation to incoming data from our senses.

Which is to say that what we *perceive* is content that our brains *create*; a construction that is the brain's best guess as to what the external world is like.

I invite you to hold onto that idea while I riff on it a little (if you feel disinclined to cut me this slack let me ask who among us can see the blind spot in our own visual field— have not our brains proactively filled in the blank?)

Suppose we wanted to build a device that operated in this perception-constructing way, in an attempt to create an artificial brain that performs with perceptual competences that are similar to those of an organic brain. In our device, the equivalent of the seat of consciousness would be the region where speculative ideas of how the world might be (e.g. images) meet and best fit the data that comes from the device's sensory apparatus.

(Let us allow that our device is some sort of three-dimensional electronic contraption. This contraption contains myriads of electronic micro-circuits, packed and wired three-dimensionally in close proximity, and immersed in coolant. The whole thing is enclosed in something the size of a shoe-box. This gives us the opportunity to think in terms of the physical arrangement of its constituents, not dissimilar to the way we might think of physical regions in a real brain. Also, keeping this shoe-box sized contraption in mind will make it easier to visualise what follows.)

At first blush we might think that the region of would-be consciousness is something of a flat cinema screen for our 'inner eye'. Of course, in fact, the screen must surround a notional centre of experience. While our visual experience might be thought of in terms of a cinema screen, our auditory experience is better thought of as 3D surround sound—we are able to position the stuff we hear in any direction in the three-dimensional space that we apparently inhabit.

So let us think not so much of a flattish cinema screen, rather let us think of the internal surface of a hollow sphere, with our supposed 'inner eye' at the centre.

This is the surface (possibly mobile, possibly dynamic—let us think of it as wobbly, impermanent, and balloon-like, about the size of a golf ball within the body of our brain-ambitioned shoe-box sized device) where the device's conjectures about the external world best fit evidence from that world.

Now, the term used for a fragment of experience is *quale* (plural *qualia*). One small patch of blue that contributes to our experience of the blue of the sky is a quale. One simple musical note that we hear amidst a complex orchestrated piece is a quale, and so on for each of our senses. Which is to say qualia come in a range of types—one type for each of our senses—and for each type there is a variety of 'flavours': reds, yellows, blues, and so on for sight; sweet, sour, bitter, and so on for taste.

The idea of the quale (at least as I use the concept in this text) is that it encapsulates some small quantity of experience; it captures both the content of the experience and the experience itself; it is the essential *what is it like?* to feel a bit of blue, or heat, or cold, or pain, or whatever.

No doubt you can see that introducing qualia does away with the 'inner eye'. The inner eye is somehow no more nor less than the sum of all qualia. And if we, in the device we are constructing, are locating the putative seat of consciousness in the spherically-ambitioned surface, then everything our device 'experiences' can only be experienced in the surface; the idea of an apparent central point of view for the device can only be inferred. There is no inner eye and any impression that one such exists needs to be accounted for in some other way.

(We cannot have an inner eye that scans the surface since the inner eye would have to have its own surface and its own inner eye and so on ad infinitum. For us, all explanation must stop at the surface and be explained in the surface or be no explanation at all.)

Resuming our quest: we must construct an external world for our device in the same way that content is generated for qualia in an organic brain. And what must that be like?

Well, we know exactly what that is like, since (if we build the thing right) it will reproduce exactly the same content that we experience; the content will be exactly the thing our [fictional] inner eye sees—not least because, consider this: the world is not in fact the way we see it. The world does not contain blue skies. The world (for instance, our earth) is surrounded by an atmosphere which emits light of certain wavelengths in certain directions which, when that light impinges on our retinas and resultant signals are processed by the brain, gives rise inside the brain to sensations of blue (or greys on a cloudy day). We know *exactly* what this experience is like; we do *not know exactly* what the world is like. The upshot being: we do know the kinds of thing our device must be capable of generating across its surface. Indeed it will be just like our inner eye's experience of its own 'cinema screen' (albeit wrap-around and three-dimensional when it comes to some sense data, and any putative experience of it is in the surface, not from a central point of view). We could even think of our device as having

LEDs in the surface which light up and paint a picture of its would-be experience just as a fully digital cinema screen might.

Because that is what *our* experience is like.

However, if our device with its 'two-dimensional' wrap-around surface aspires to be brain-like (to demonstrate that in principle this approach to brain design would plausibly work), there are three major problems to address.

First, how can a three-dimensional world be understood by experience in a two-dimensional surface without introducing a second 'viewer' who is going to interpret all the visual depth cues from shapes (like perspective), from sounds (like stereoscopic hearing), from sensations (like an extended arm), and from whatever else contributes to the apparently three-dimensional manifestation of *our* experience?

Second, there is the question of how anything so generated can be instantiated in the surface and mean something—can have its own meaning. How can the sight of the sky be understood beyond our experience of the colour blue i.e. to exist in our minds as part of the sky? Is not every real perception imbued with additional information that is not obviously part of what we perceive?

Third, how can the passage of time be perceived in the surface without an observer who can notice the difference between one moment and the next, to observe change in the felt experience of the world and deduce *Aha! Time has passed!* To introduce any such observer undermines our attempt to construct (and indeed explain) a properly constituted, content-creating device (be it conscious or unconscious).

Perception of time is the primary interest of this piece, so I will leave the questions of dimension, meaning, and indeed the question of individual quale generation for another occasion, except to say that qualia have duration. They are not instantaneous. I.e. they do not exist for a moment so infinitesimally short that they can hardly be said to last any time at all.

It must be true to say that qualia last a noticeable length of time (but that's not to say much).

Let us return to what our brain-ambitioned device is doing while all this content generating is going on. The device is creating speculations about what the world is like, comparing those speculations to perhaps a paucity of data arriving from its sensory apparatus, and rendering into perceived experience its best speculative guess as to what the world is like.

We perceive the external world as a uniform, continuous and for the most part smooth-running whole. In order for our device to generate an impression of uniformity, continuity, and so on, the speculative component of the device will need, all the time, to be anticipating changes in the external world (the moving cloud, the approaching person, the police siren wailing in the distance). It must present these anticipations to the surface as weak or dilute additional content, so that when the world changes as the device anticipates, the transition in content is from dilute to dense, from weak to strong, as the speculatively anticipated content is reinforced because it better matches evidence newly arrived from the sensory apparatus.

Why, you might ask, must the smooth transition be between the now and an anticipated future rather than merely rely on the slow decay of the present representation of the world as the associated qualia fade? The answer is that if a brain (or our device) does not anticipate what is going to happen next, then every change in the field of view (or hearing or whatever other of the senses) must be evaluated as if new and fresh, whereas anticipated behaviour is something which can easily be inserted from memories of past experience, thereby doing part of the work in advance. Additionally, for any living creature, there is a survival advantage in the predictive approach. If an animal brain is constantly predicting what will happen next it will be easier to notice differences between what is predicted and the way the world turns out, which in turn will alert the animal to unexpected threats. A creature whose brain predictively generates content will thus have a survival advantage (a speedier response for less energy consumed) over a creature that is merely reactive to the external world (i.e. evolutionary pressure will favour a predictive brain).

One moment the world is this way (say, I am striking a match) and yet at the same time, our device is painting, albeit indistinctly, what it anticipates is likely to come next. Most of the time what the device anticipates will happen, happens (there is a burst of flame); old qualia fade; new qualia come into being and supersede them; there is overlap and continuity. Content in the surface evidences no reason to question or scrutinize or doubt the way the world is; the brain's correct understanding of the world, illustrated by the continuously changing content in the surface, is endorsed with every moment that passes.

You might say that for a second time our device proactively meets evidence from the external world half-way: first it speculates, then it anticipates.

However the upshot is: our would-be qualia-producing surface does not perceive time. The surface as the seat of consciousness is forever transitioning, and for the most part smoothly, because of the freshly, predictively generated content.

Time is the ghost of the next thing that might happen.

(The concept *Time* and all talk of time are relegated to the spoken or unspoken word, to reason and ratiocination. Words are only sounds, or ghosts of sounds, and while they must acquire meaning solely via the surface, the unravelling of meaning for words demands a separate approach from the unravelling of the experience of time described here.)

But my experience is simply not like that! You might say.

So let me invite you to a little pseudo-meditation.

I invite you to sit still and contemplate the world around you. I invite you to focus on the senses; to put to one side the unspoken flow of words that are your ongoing internal ratiocinations; to hold still, aware of what is around you and ask yourself at any moment in time how much of what I am aware of do I have to understand, to identify—assign meaning to—from one moment to the next? I invite you to entertain the thought that it is not so much that you articulate in the moment everything you know about everything around you in your current circumstance, rather you are comfortable not having to worry about the noises coming from outside, or the nature of the window, or the fact that the desk you are leaning on is in fact a desk. A degree of unalarmed acceptance is present across the whole of your perceptual field. The world is as it is, and is in no need of inquisition. If anything, the one and only thing you do notice is unexpected change.

Following this brief meditation, absent any and all sub-vocalisations, perhaps the idea that *time is the ghost of the next thing that might happen* does not seem so wild?

Time is one piece in the jigsaw of our experience of the world which any theory of consciousness must give an account of. Other major pieces in the jigsaw that require explanation are meaning, an appreciation of spacial depth, language, and qualia themselves. Each of these can be accounted for in the surface without having to resort to an inner eye, which of course we cannot appeal to since an inner eye explains nothing. But those accounts do not belong here.

At the start of this text I asked *How do we perceive time?* The answer is, we don't. The surface presents a unified, smoothly continuous experience of an apparent external world. No more, no less. We can talk of time, sure. But talk of time is not the same as perceiving time. *Time is...* well, I think you know the rest by now.

Death of a Homunculus

WHAT'S YOUR FAVORITE movie?

Maybe it's *Titanic* or *The Godfather*; maybe something from *Star Wars* or *The Shawshank Redemption*; maybe *Chinatown*, *Blade Runner*, *Schindler's List*, or *Pulp Fiction*[44].

Of all the movies you've ever seen, which comes to mind?

As you summon up the essence of it, what scenes or sounds, music or mood play back across the movie screen of your mind's eye?

What lingers?

Now, please hold onto that image, sound, scene, or mood, like a freeze frame, as if the meaning of the whole ninety minute experience is captured in that one moment, frozen in time...

WHEN ASKED WHAT makes a good movie, the actress, comedienne, screenwriter, and singer Rosalind Russell (1907-1976) said: "Moments. A couple of moments that people remember, that they can take with them."[45]

---

44 Titanic, 1997 Dir. James Cameron, The Godfather, 1972 Dir. Francis Ford Coppola, Star Wars, 1977 Dir. George Lucas, The Shawshank Redemption, 1994 Dir. Frank Darabont, Chinatown, 1974 Dir Roman Polanski, Blade Runner, 1982 Dir. Ridley Scott, Schindler's List, 1993, Dir. Steven Spielberg, Pulp Fiction, 1994, Dir. Quentin Tarantino (source: www.IMDB.com)

45 Sources: Raymond Obstfeld's "Novelist's Essential Guide to Crafting Scenes", Writer's Digest Books, 17 Aug. 2000, ch 1, and https://www.bestmoviesbyfarr.com/articles/rosalind-russell/2019/07.

Let us examine the moment. The one you're holding on pause in your mind's eye.

The emphasis will be different for each of us, of course. Some of us are visually oriented creatures, some of us audiophiles, and for some of us it's all about emotional intensity: whether it's love won or lost, or the excitement of the chase, or perhaps it's about Justice and seeing Right done.

Whichever has grabbed you, you have conjured up some essence of your favorite movie and it lives again within you, freeze-framed in your mind's eye.

And my question is: How does it come to mean what it does to you?

Now, I'm not asking the question of whether you saw the movie on the occasion of your (unforgettable) n^{th} birthday, or in the company of the unforgettable *whoever*, or on the same day as thus-and-such world-shattering event. My inquiry is about what internally is going on in our minds that allows us to understand the scene we have freeze-framed: how do our minds give meaning to what our memory has served up?

"What's so difficult about that?" You might say. "In the movie, you told a powerful story. Through characters and events you connected it to my life. I have strong associations with what I have seen and heard on-screen. These things affect me because they use just enough of what is familiar to me for me to suspend my disbelief. That's what movies are designed to do!"

Still (if your answer is along those lines) I persist with my question, to pin you down; I am after the internal mental process that endows the moment with meaning. How is the mind's eye able to give meaning to what is now on your inner, subjective movie screen?

Likely as not you reach for the word you reached for before, and repeat it to me, fool that I am: "Associations!"

NOW LET US return to the movie theater and the big screen itself.

In terms of a theater, I have in mind a simple setup: a flat screen and no 3D effects (OK, maybe we can have surround sound. You are allowed a little luxury).

There we sit in the auditorium, in more or less comfort, listening to the rustle and scratch of pop corn and the frenetic bipping of mobile phones before they are rendered silent. The air is both sweet and stale and the tang of pine-scented polish lingers after what must be days since the last shine—and yet, and yet—there is electricity in the air: a frisson of excitement, a tingle of anticipation for the journey to come...

The house lights fade to near-black orange.

The guillotine slice of a stock sound effect leads into the booming bass of the first advert to penetrate the dark.

Bold geometric shapes are projected onto the screen[46].

We watch (enthralled, indifferent, or embarrassed—you decide) as a jet black truck, a metal monster with four wheel drive, crunches its way up a steep incline, bronco-bucking over a heat-hazed gravel track toward a perfect cerulean blue sky. We understand the three-dimensional world to which the scene belongs. We tie together the sounds and the music and the on-screen images; we catch the mood—one of freedom, physical challenge and sensory pleasure; and we make sense of the scene before us; the advert successfully conveys a microcosm of the world (albeit a microcosm of a fictional world that the advertiser wants us to yearn for).

But how, exactly, do we construct this world in our heads from a two-dimensional screen, i.e. to make sense of it?[47]

Indeed are we constructing an internal three-dimensional representation (or model) of the world? Well, maybe we are, but if we are, do we not need another mind to make sense of what is now represented in our heads in three dimensions? We do not perceive both the 2D view and the 3D view. Our consciousness does not range over different modelings of the world; we simply perceive the world as a unified continuous thing and that's the end of our perceiving (memory and imagination notwithstanding; for those we must vary the narrative a little).

---

46 I said it was old-school.

47 Standard depth cues such as binocular vision or focal distance are not available to us, so all the depth information is contained in the images on the two-dimensional screen plus any sound effects coming from wherever the loudspeakers are. We can use cues from our experience or knowledge of perspective, of course. The cinematographer might have done tricks with focal depth, and distant objects will be less vivid than those close to (and the sound of more distant objects quieter).

In our mind's eye we perceive what is out there (*Look! There it is now, on-screen!*), but who or what is making sense of what we are perceiving?

If we invoke a second mind to make sense of the first, will we not need to invoke a third to make sense of what the second perceives, and so on, ad infinitum?

We end up with an infinite set of nested minds (like Russian Dolls, but more so).

This idea of requiring one mind inside another to solve the (difficult) problems of the first is an example of what we can call a *homunculus*.

The inner mind is the homunculus and it provides a kind of cheat that will solve any problem for us when we try to explain the mind that is nextwise outer to it. The term derives from the historical case of The Mechanical Turk, which was a chess-playing hoax dating from 1770. An apparently miraculous chess-playing cabinet was in fact operated by a small man concealed inside. In this instance he was the homunculus[48].

Ultimately, our explanation cannot rest on an infinity of minds inside each of our heads (the cranium being of finite size). Aside from anything else, this infinity explains nothing.

Perceiving, a homunculean task

Figure 1. An infinite regress of homunculi.

---

48 wikipedia: https://en.wikipedia.org/wiki/Mechanical_Turk

However, it turns out the homunculus is a phenomenon we will have difficulty eliminating. It raises its head with unwelcome regularity when it comes to matters of the mind[49].

Alternatively, when it comes to the problem above, of understanding what is on-screen: perhaps the image is broken down into its component parts, each with its own meaning. Here a tree; there a track. Here a shiny black truck; there a cloudless blue sky...

And yet, if we break the image before us down into its component parts in order to understand the things that constitute it, how do we perceive the scene as a whole? Once more we have solved one problem only to create another. As suggested above: we perceive a unified whole, not a collage of parts (Figure 2).

Sheep in field with hedge and tree:

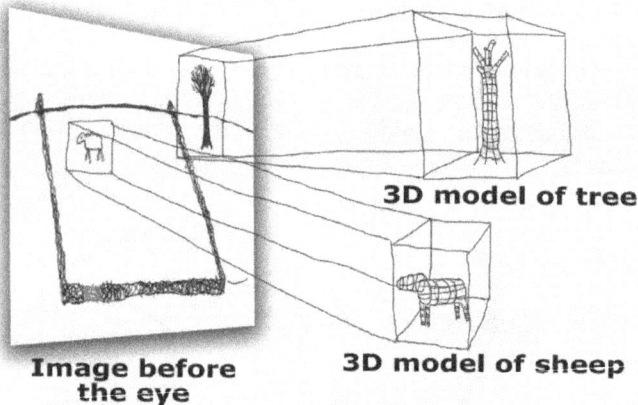

Figure 2. Sheep in field with hedge and tree. An image might be disassembled into three-dimensional component parts, but these parts are not what we perceive.

AT THIS POINT let me introduce the Lock Step model of consciousness.

The Lock Step model makes no claim to represent how the brain in fact works. Rather it offers an explanation of how a physical brain *might* work to solve the difficulties

49 It lurks inside questions like What makes us conscious? and How do we perceive meaning, depth, and time?

above, as well as tackling various other difficulties we come across when we try to explain our mental life[50].

The Lock Step model envisages two processes that run in opposite directions across a brain-like substrate[51]. The process running left-to-right conveys data (or signals) from the sense organs and, as these signals travel to the right, they are sieved for recognizable patterns, most trivially (say): edges, ovals and rectangles.

At the same time, another process is running right-to-left across the same brain-like substrate. Coming from the right the second process conveys impressions of concepts and ideas[52], and as it conveys these impressions to the left, the concepts are refined and made more specific. Moreover, concepts coming from the right are speculative; they are a best guess at the likely content of the world that we currently perceive, given the current world context[53].

For instance, a very general representation of the concept 'vehicle', during the process of being conveyed from the right toward the left, might be modified to include wheels, to become more specific, as evidence from the left accrues (for instance, the prior more general concept of vehicle as a mobile carrier, regardless of means of propulsion or support, might have encompassed the hovercraft).

The two processes (let us call one sensory and the other conceptual) overlap across the whole of the substrate, but there will be a region where the data (or signals) carried by the sensory process from the left match the speculative concepts coming from the right.

In the Lock Step model we say that the seat of consciousness is where the two signals best match.

Of course, the two signals can match in more than one place, so the Lock Step model also requires the seat of

---

50 The Lock Step model and how it might be implemented mechanically, i.e. using something other than a human brain, is described in depth in "The Man in My Head Has Lost His Mind", Logic of Dreams, 2023, and "This Robot Brain Gets Life", Logic of Dreams, 2023.

51 In real brains neurons are uni-directional dendrite-to-axon, which is one reason why this is NOT like a real brain substrate.

52 For those with a philosophical background one might draw (loose) parallels with Plato's forms.

53 If you are up a mountain you might expect to see a mountain goat; if you are in the middle of town you might expect to see a stray dog.

consciousness to shift as far right as it can, to settle in the region of maximum 'meaning.' 'Meaning' here indicates the highest order conceptual view that is consistent with the available evidence from the incoming sensory signal.

As an example: a Ford pickup truck is both a better candidate for perceived reality than a collection of rectangles, ovals and lines (patterns in data from the retina, coming from the left), and also a better match than some generic four-wheel drive vehicle (coming from the right). So Ford it must be[54].

One way to visualize the Lock Step model is as a shallow tray containing two immiscible oils, one red and one blue. The red oil sits on the left hand side of the tray, and represents processes carrying sensory data (left to right). The blue oil sits at the right hand side of the tray and represents processes bearing concepts and abstract ideas (right to left). The two meet somewhere near the middle of the tray and the junction is shaped like a vertical ribbon (Figure 3).

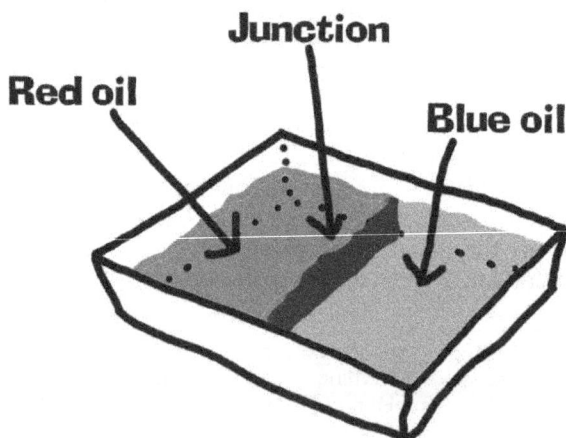

Figure 3. The Lock Step oil tray metaphor.

---

54 You might say the only choice is a Ford. BTW I don't get sponsorship for this, but if someone wanted to contact me...

In this metaphor, the junction is the seat of consciousness and can shift to and fro as the oils move[55]. Thus conscious focus of attention is visualised as moving between more and less precise (or less and more general) representations of the things and stuffs speculated as being present in the world[56].

What's the point of all this?

Essentially, to suggest that our understanding (and awareness) arises where a brain process of speculation meets a process that sieves sensory data for patterns.

This offers the prospect of ridding ourselves of the homunculus. We are solving the problem of identifying and understanding objects within our field of view while at the same time maintaining the sense of a unified movie screen effect for our mind's eye.

Except, we have not in fact removed the homunculus problem.

One job of the homunculus was to take the flat planar view of the movie theater screen and render it as an understandable 3D world inside our heads.

In the Lock Step model we have done no more than reproduce the movie screen as the ribbon of consciousness, albeit making some added meaning available in principle via the right-to-left speculative data stream.

There must be more of a story to tell...

Enter QUALIA stage right, grinning smugly.

The technical term for an instance of our subjective perceived experience—a splash of orange in a sunset; a single note played on a trombone; a burst of saltiness as one closes ones lips over an olive—is a *quale*. Plural *qualia*.

Our perceived visual field could be said to be comprised of a myriad of qualia, as could any other of our sensory fields (being regions where sensations apparently arise).

We have different kinds of qualia for different senses, and for each of those senses we may receive qualia in a variety of flavors[57]. Visual qualia can arise in reds, yellows,

---

55 This is a thought experiment, so the oils can magically be kept level.

56 Things are objects: dogs, cats, toasters, houses. Stuff are materials: water, butter, and cooking oil. Things are indivisible. Stuffs are can be divided and remain the same stuff.

57 We must watch our language here: technically speaking

purples and so on. Auditory qualia can arise in high and low tones, and anything in between[58]. And while visual and auditory qualia may appear to have a position in a perceptual field (positioned relative to other qualia on the movie screen of our mind's eye; the blue sky is above the gravel track, and so on), some qualia, such as rage and fear are all-consuming and swamp the whole of our perceived world[59].

Philosophically, the notions of quale and qualia are not without difficulty[60], but the Lock Step model uses them in a particular way.

With reference to the oil tray, qualia are generated where the two oils meet. And while the oil tray model is a metaphor, and somewhat removed from any reality, the metaphor can be transformed into a real, physical machine, which is exactly what is described, in detail, in the book "This Robot Brain Gets Life" [RBGL] (Logic of Dreams, 2023).

RBGL posits a brain-like machine consisting of functional blocks like Memory and Perception (where incoming signals from the senses are sieved for patterns) and, importantly, a Sandbox block (called *Ideation*) where concepts can be formed and compared to patterns obtained from the Perception block.

Importantly also: the brain-like machine in RBGL is everything we humans might be, although it is only conscious when instantiated in a flesh and blood brain.

In RBGL, the ribbon of consciousness in the oil tray metaphor morphs into a closed two-dimensional Surface not unlike the inside of a hollow sphere, although it does not have to be particularly spherical[61].

I invite you to imagine, if you will, a hollow sphere lined with a thin, qualia-producing layer. This is our Surface. Let

---

we don't experience qualia; qualia are the experience.

58 Although for us humans the available tones may be limited by the positioning of hairs in our inner ear i.e. what wavelength of sound those hairs resonate to.

59 Some fiction writers might like to locate these two in the gut. I leave you to judge for yourself the next time you are afflicted by one such emotion.

60 Source, wikipedia: https://en.wikipedia.org/wiki/Qualia

61 The Surface does not need to occupy a fixed location in the brain-like machine, nor does it need to adopt any particular shape. The only constraint on shape is that a straight line may be drawn from any one point on the surface to the notional center of the space enclosed by the surface without crossing the surface.

us suppose that auditory qualia can be generated at any location across the whole of the Surface, whereas visual qualia may only be generated in a region taken to be the 'forward' direction. Direction and orientation are imposed on the sphere by the body to which it belongs. In particular the location of the sense of smell is fixed and limited[62].

Upon waking, for any living, breathing creature in possession of a brain like this, the Surface bursts into life and generates qualia that represent the creature's brain's best guess at what the world before it is like.

The qualia are both the content of and constitutive of perceived experience. Here we have the movie screen of the mind's eye—except there is no 'mind's eye'; there is only The Surface.

One immediate question is: what direction do qualia face? Why do we suppose (as seems natural to suppose) they implicitly face inward, toward some notional center point of the (closed and spherically-ambitioned) Surface? Why should they?

In RBGL we suggest that facing inward is the lowest energy state for the physics that underpins them. So we have them facing inward, what next?

We have painted a picture (as it were) in qualia across the inside of The Surface, how now do we imbue that experience with understanding? How do we give anything that is perceived in this way any Meaning? Indeed, how are we to convey depth or time through a two-dimensional surface (i.e. without a homunculus to make such judgements for us about what's on the surface)?

Remember, The Surface is all we have. There is nothing more to perception. Everything we understand must be understood *in* the Surface, as perceived. If we try to process the picture we have painted in any way, we re-introduce the homunculus. Notably, we cannot perceive depth (for which a 3D model would be required); we cannot perceive time (for

---

62 The Surface is embedded in the brain substrate which we now think of as a three-dimensional brain-like goo. Also, the Surface need not be fixed to any one location in our 3D substrate —it could wander and change shape (if there were a fixed structure like that in a physical brains, I'm sure that ancient Greek, and Roman, physicians would have noticed). Although Descartes' ascribing the seat of consciousness [the soul] to the pineal gland appears now somewhat more profound than one at first might have thought.

ongoing memory comparisons would be required, yet our perception is 'of the moment'), and we have no access to Meaning (We might be able to give ourselves a running commentary of things and events in the world, but a running commentary is merely a sequence of phonemes; there being no homunculus to hear it).

It would seem that the Lock Step model, by presenting us with the Surface, has made itself the hostage of all time to the homunculus!

Except, no.

And this is where a sentient creature whose brain is an instance of the Lock Step model is different from a mechanical device which instantiates the exact same model.

The sentient creature will have qualia where the mechanical device might, at its most garish, have color LEDs[63].

The sentient creature is capable of feelings which are simply not available to the mechanical device, not merely and most obviously pain, but also *Meaning(M)*.

RBGL posits Meaning as a particular feeling of satisfaction or confidence. The feeling of Meaning can arise anywhere in The Surface, and the feeling accompanies any qualia-generating content for which the brain can deliver a sufficiency of corroborative evidence. Corroborative evidence might arise from a good correspondence between data from the senses and data from memory in the context of everything else that apparently constitutes the brain's current world view.

Positing a feeling of Meaning (or if it makes it easier to think about it: a feeling of some observed image or sound's *having a meaning*) may sound like a cheat, but it is the same species of feeling as when we speak of the difference in feeling when we claim we know thus-and-such as opposed to merely think thus-and-such, or *guess* thus-and-such. The feeling of Meaning is that extra confidence, or conviction of rightness—of verisimilitude[64].

If the brain indicates through qualia of Meaning that some object in The Surface is 'good' then we, the perceiver, are untroubled by it. In particular we give special attention[65]

---

63 Or whatever is today's lighting device of choice.
64 The feeling might be incorrect; the brain can be wrong yet convinced.
65 To be clear: the physical brain drives attention. Qualia in

to wherever the feeling of Meaning is not present—in evolutionary terms the unknown and unrecognized may conceal a threat to survival.

If the (unperceived) mechanism of the brain indicates a high degree of confidence in the shape, size, location or orientation in the real, physical world of (say) the Ford truck that intrudes upon our visual field, then that's good enough for The Surface: *say no more!* The Surface in the moment does not need to know, homunculus-like, that it is a Ford truck. If the brain for whatever reason changes the focus of attention to the truck, and embarks on an internal monologue about the history of trucks, The Surface will receive a series of words, possibly accompanied by associated images from memory, all of which will have Meaning (in the feeling sense) but all of which exist only in the moment[66] [67].

Fine, say you (perhaps): we can do the same for establishing depth in the Surface. 'Invent'—*why don't you*— some qualia to signify depth, and issue them in response to the brain's estimation of how far away the Ford truck is... But no. We cannot do that because if we provide the Surface with depth information who or what is going to process that information? (Figure 4.)

The homunculus, that's who[68].

The trick when it comes to depth perception is to realize:

First, we have more than the five senses so often cited. Not only do we have sight, sound, taste, smell, and touch. We also have pain and balance and hunger and thirst and some sense of how our limbs move and are positioned (proprioception). (There are other senses too.)

---

the Surface merely re-present the brain's best guess at what the world is like. There is still the opportunity for cause and effect from qualia to brain states (pleasure, pain and the rest can end up in memory), but the Surface is not a homunculus conducting affairs like a General.

66 There is the question of how short-term memory works. But this too, can be orchestrated by the brain, which can bring what it mechanically decides (and is capable of) to The Surface.

67 This is not to say The Surface plays no causal role in events, merely that, as per MIMH, causality will have to be indirect, mediated by memory, and a response to the piquancy that is added to content by feeling. MIMH Chapter 7. Evolution and Free Will.

68 We can't simply issue the data to The Surface and declare: 'here it is; you've got all you need; deal with it!'

And second: our memories include behaviors, such as the sight of an animal scratching, or a tree falling.

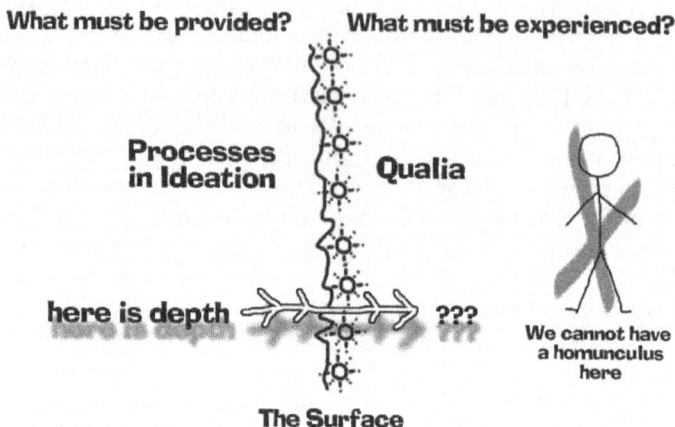

What must be provided?   What must be experienced?

Processes in Ideation   Qualia

here is depth   ???

We cannot have a homunculus here

The Surface

Figure 4. How can depth be conveyed through the Surface in a way that needs no further processing or understanding?

RBGL presents behaviors as sequences of changes in the (two-dimensional) shape of a thing, or patterns of tonal variations in the noises it makes[69]. A domino may fall; we see it slant to one side (say) and its height reduces, frame by frame as it were, until it ends up flat on its spotty face.

In The Surface we say that the next potential frame of behavior of every object is presented as a ghost of itself, and without Meaning. That is: the brain injects into The Surface an anticipated next frame for all things and stuffs in the observed world. However in terms of perception, the contents of the frame of anticipated data is weak. Indeed truly ghost-like. Perhaps for every 100 micro qualia giving rise to a patch of orange in our sunset, two or three micro qualia anticipate the gray of the encroaching cloud.

Of course we do not—cannot—perceive a transition from one moment to the next; that would be to summon the homunculus. No, what the presence of the anticipated next frame does is to smooth the transition from one moment to the next[70].

---

69 Or color or any other sensory change.
70 RBGL postulates that qualia, though short-lived, are not

One moment we have the ghost of a cloud. The next moment we have the gray of a cloud which is endorsed by the feeling of Meaning. We have continuity. And so long as we have continuity, our perception of the world is of one continuous, unified whole[71]. The brain does not signal, nor the Surface announce, any discontent.

If we don't have continuity, our brain is already—before we even notice—struggling to make sense of what must be wrong...

How does behavior help explain how The Surface can perceive depth? Firstly through what an object in the world might do ('behave' as in *change*) and second through what we might do ('behave' as in *perform*).

An object, like a tree, can exhibit falling down behavior, which the brain will have access to from Memory. If the brain assesses the falling down behavior of the tree as likely, it can paint the first (or next) frame of tree behavior into The Surface.

But there is also our behavior. From birth, we explore the world and learn. We use our fingers to prod things. We use our legs to travel (and fall over). We gain an appreciation of the space through which we can and do move. And our appreciation is to some extent understood through the mechanics of our limbs; fingers for small scale; walking for a larger scale. These are all felt things, and these felt things— the actuations and the impacts of our personal behavior— can be painted into The Surface as ghostly anticipations.

The brain will serve up the most likely behaviors and The Surface will have expectations that are met and feel continuous (or not) and 'all is right with the world' (or not) as behaviors play out in the world and Meaning is asserted.

To recap: for some item in the Surface to have Meaning, the brain has located a sufficiency of associations to that item in Memory, or Perception, or conceptually or in the current world context that the brain can assert a degree of confidence in the verisimilitude of that item.

For The Surface to perceive depth, possible future depth cues are presented as ghostly perceptions, which if borne out by what happens next (and Meaning is asserted) merely

---

instantaneous things. They do not have an infinitely short duration.

71 Timewise, at least.

present a smoothly changing, continuous world (perceptual ghosts can come and go and hardly be noticed).

That leaves us with the problem of capturing time in the Surface.

The Surface cannot perceive time.

But we have already answered our question: Our perception of time can only be the ghost of what might happen next[72].

We never perceive the whole; we perceive steps on the way to the whole; each step may be endorsed by the brain as moment to moment the brain asserts Meaning—like steps in mathematical proof which is never understood all at once, but we readily endorse each step on its own[73].

EARLIER I SUGGESTED that while audio qualia may be generated anywhere on the Surface, visual qualia will be limited to a notional forward direction[74]. However, this is not the correct picture. Since we can visualize (imagine) things and stuffs behind us, out of sight, there must be a sufficient density of visual qualia everywhere across the surface to support imagery to whatever extent our individual imaginations allow[75].

The overall picture is more like Figure 5.

In Figure 5 we see the relative densities of regions of the Surface ahead of and rearward of the notional centre of perception (being careful to note that perception occurs only in, and is integral to, the Surface. There is no 'central viewpoint' to experience, or adopt (a central viewpoint would require a homunculus)).

---

72 For a full explanation of the Lock Step model, it is introduced in MIMH and elaborated enough to instantiate it in RBGL.

73 Given A and B it follows that C. Given C and D it follows that E. But we may never hold the whole proof in our heads, as a single thought, that A and B and D necessitate E.

74 Relative to the head, tethered to the location of the sense of smell.

75 It is a moot point as to whether, by developing the imagination, one could increase one's potential qualia-producing density anywhere in the Surface. We are told the brain is plastic; that individuals can learn to 'perceive' through implants; so I'm thinking: *why not?*

Cross section, front-to-rear, through the Surface

Region of high
resolution and
high qualia
density

Region of low
resolution and
low qualia
density

cluster A
cluster B
cluster C
cluster D
cluster E
cluster F

cluster P

cluster Q

cluster R

(*qualia originate
in neural clusters
under the right conditions*)

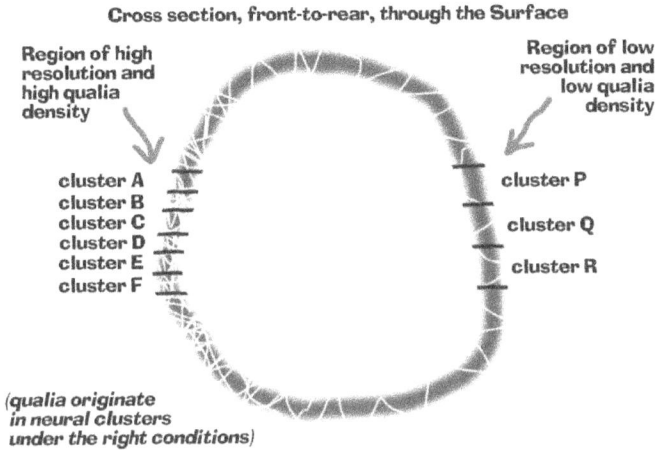

Figure 5. Audio and visual qualia are generated across the whole Surface, but the visual qualia generation is not evenly distributed.

THE PICTURE I have painted is of a closed Surface where a two-dimensional guess at what the world is like plays out and receives more or less credence against evidence that comes from the senses, and memory, and cogitations[76].

The Surface does not have to be in a fixed location in the brain[77]—indeed one might envisage it as the inside face of a wobbly balloon-like thing (like *Rover* in The Prisoner[78]) which changes shape as it moves as would a bouncing beach ball made of jelly.

In sentient creatures, the Surface is the seat of consciousness and the source of qualia.

So far I have said next to nothing about causality.

If the production of qualia plays no role in the operation of the brain i.e. cannot cause changes in the brain, then consciousness is a mere side-effect of the mechanical activity of the brain and that mechanical activity could be replicated by any suitably configured machine.

---

76 Mental reasoning in the form of language or symbols.

77 If there was any such fixed structure I'm sure that ancient Greek and Roman surgeons would have noticed.

78 The Prisoner was a 1967 cult British television series starring, written, and directed by Patrick McGoohan. Rover was a balloon-like perimeter guard.

The argument from MIMH is that consciousness evolved, and that any creature that is conscious has an evolutionary advantage over one that is not. Love and pain and fear and the rest confer that advantage, which means that they must play a causal role in the activity of the brain and mind.

For reasons set out in MIMH, the causal element is not the immediacy that one might assume, i.e. of "I will do this thing here and now." Rather, qualia, as they come into and go out of existence, affect how memories are stored. The causal role of consciousness is not 'in the moment' so much as 'in the memory' (pain, fear etc.) of previous moments, and ongoing cogitations.

However, it is important that it is causal, and via memory, and that particular feelings, sensations, and emotions can be reproduced via memories (at the very least, memory storage must be affected by consciousness).

In RBGL we construct a machine that reproduces the Surface, but instead of generating qualia (which only a living brain can do) Surface content is parametrized as if qualia were being produced and those parameters are stored in Memory alongside sense-data content (The aim was to design a machine capable of 'understanding' and 'concept formation' while also being honest and moral).

So one might ask: if we can parametrize content to simulate the effects of qualia on brain function, what makes that different from what a real brain is, in effect, doing? Why are we not thereby simulating everything the brain is doing and arriving at a mechanical brain which exactly simulates the physical operation and physical effects of the human brain-mind complex?

Which is a good question and one for which we might try to lean on complexity[79] for an answer.

One might envisage calculating the motions of all the particles that make up the surface but for the fact that such a calculation would be so astronomically large as to require more resources than are available in the known universe. Only Nature can solve a problem of such complexity—not by simulation, but by operating the real thing: a real brain. Nothing simpler can produce the same results; nor can

---

79 A version of chaos theory in fact. About limits on computability.

anything having the same level of complexity as the brain[80] be computed.

Only a living brain can do what a living brain does (and that involves real qualia).

Except that argument is insufficient.

Suppose the test for effective qualia substitution (i.e. using parameters in our artificial brain where feeling would arise in a real brain) is survival and the will to survive. If we assign a number to some strength of feeling on some occasion (let us say of pain) and let that number be "7.5", suppose that the actual, felt pain is properly represented by some number close to "7.5" but which is a so-called *irrational* number[81]. We cannot calculate the exact number, but we can say that if we amplify our parametrized equivalent very slightly it will provide greater motivation to act than the motivation provided by the real pain.

If parameters are all we rely on, our mechanical brain can be configured to out-perform our flesh-and-blood brains.

This is both intuitively uncomfortable (are we saying qualia are worth nothing to us?) and intellectually does not tally with the idea that consciousness evolved because it delivered a survival advantage.

To deliver a survival advantage, it must be causal. It must make a difference and that difference must depend on the unique quality that it brings with it.

When we recall a painful memory, we are able to regenerate and re-experience the pain; who does not grimace even now at some long past incident, perhaps at school, that one would much rather forget? The grimace is more than a parametrized incentive[82] not to repeat some pattern of behaviour. And yet how does the feeling connect to the brain that supports the Surface if not by sending real, physical electro-chemical signals that are indeed capable of being recorded and even reproduced (artificially if need be)?

---

80 I.e. down to the atomic level.

81 Irrational numbers are real numbers that cannot be expressed by the fraction of two integers. 7.5 is rational because it can be expressed as 75 / 10. Pi is irrational because there is no single fraction that exactly captures it

82 We could have a whole calculus of incentives once we parametrized all our feelings, which is, sort of what RBGL is all about in the quest to build in alignment and design hallucination out.

There is a temptation to re-introduce the homunculus. To say that, on the qualia-side of things, in The Surface, the co-existence of certain patterns of qualia produces some additional effect, provides strength or reinforcement or longevity of a quale which is not available other than through some field-effect in the field of qualia.

In MIMH we posited the *gleeon* as a fundamental particle that existed in a universal gleeon field. And in RBGL we argued that for a Surface in a brain to present a unified sense of self, micro-qualia production must be sufficiently dense that they act together, in some sort of resonance, to form a continuous Surface.

Which is to say, we already have it that qualia on a Surface are connected field-wise. And so long as no mechanical or computative work is required of the field of qualia (or activated gleeons that underpin them) then the secret advantage that the animal brain has over the mechanical brain might still be an incalculable (and uncalculating) resonance that consciousness alone can achieve, or brings with it[83].

NOW THAT WE have established a model for consciousness and shown that it is causative and cannot be reproduced by a machine, we return to questions of Art and Authenticity.

We might suggest that Art is Authentic if it communicates feelings to its audience; it is Authentic if both creator and consumer are feeling creatures who connect via their felt aesthetic sensibilities[84] [85].

---

83 Arguably, this field effect might be calculated, and simulated; possibly other brains could evolve without consciousness but with the calculating apparatus. Although, clearly consciousness is a simpler mechanism and would have evolutionary advantage. But the idea of a calculating equivalent is still unattractive—except I would say that because consciousness has an attraction all of its own, don't you think?

84 I do not present this as a definition in any strong sense, because the word aesthetic smuggles in the idea of Art. It is more of an elaboration of the idea of Art.

85 And of course that the Artist hold true to soul, self, beliefs and so on—that kind of Authentic too

I think this will serve as a good starting point. We have drawn a boundary around the field in which we shall play— We have the size of our canvas; the word-count for our text; the budget for our orchestra... *and mixed metaphors to boot!*

The Net-Hook Fallacy

RECENTLY, I WAS introduced to a man who saved schools.

These were failing schools, you understand. Schools which the authorities had decided had gone so badly wrong that external intervention was needed. Maybe it was bad exam results, non-existent discipline, or a health and safety catastrophe. They would send this guy in.

But he did not do the obvious. If exam results were poor, he did not spend his budget on recruiting new teachers or buying new equipment; if discipline was poor, he did not throw money at drawing up tighter rules, employing extra staff to police every move of every student, nor to fund out-of-hours detentions—or other punishments; if health and safety fell short, he did not send all the staff on health and safety courses, and police the corridors with jobsworths.

No. Not at all.

In every case he distributed the rescue budget funds equitably and generally. He invested equally in every aspect of the school. He aimed to raise the whole, not target the obvious symptoms. This is what worked. He was a long-established professional in the job and had a strong track record. He did not *Band-aid* the wound, nor operate on the damaged limb. He improved the health of the body as a whole.

ANY SOCIETY IS a complex entity. A city, even the most dysfunctional city, is a miracle of co-operation and interaction. There are many services which work alongside each other and are integrated. No one activity dominates. All are interlinked and interdependent. So much so that the whole could be described relative to, and in terms of, any one of its parts.

You could put the city hospital on a pedestal and describe everything else in the city in relation to it.

7% of the city's workforce are employed directly by the hospital. Another 7% as sub-contractors and another 5% interact in some way with the hospital itself, be it postal services, social services, or telecoms providers. As for the rest of the workforce, they provide the infrastructure that makes the hospital possible. Not forgetting the 85% of city residents who visit the hospital in some capacity at some time or other in their lives.

And if you look hard enough you will find that every worker in the city does indeed work to a greater or lesser extent in support of the hospital and its direct employees. Hospital workers must be fed: we have food shops and restaurants. Hospital workers must have homes: we have housing—home ownership and landlords, and associated regulations and civic and legal services. Can the hospital workers get to work? We have public transport, and private transport and then construction and maintenance services to support those. And on it goes...

What do workers at the hospital need to support the effective and efficient running of the hospital? Answer: everything that a city normally provides.

However, since the city is an integrated whole, and everything is linked to everything else, the same argument can be made for any sector of city activity: lawyers, accountants, construction workers, musicians, hairdressers, road traffic cops, and politicians...

Of course the truth is, all these roles and the aspects of city life to which they belong are needed. Not one of them is more important[86] than any other when it comes to the smooth mechanistic functioning of the city[87].

---

86 Functional importance should not be confused with the cost of purchasing a skill or talent, or the human value of an individual life. Doctors may be paid more because they are a rarer commodity (in economic terms) or have invested more of their lives (in personal terms) and money (in family commitment terms) in training, or have abilities which are rare (in psychological terms) and obviously precious to society (in societal aspirational terms). I.e. the point I'm making is silent when it comes to the party politics of the city.

87 Even the philosophers, if they go on strike, inconvenience

And in terms of the smooth functioning of the city, no one activity should be elevated in its importance or in the demands it can make with regard to the rest. If the network of the city's interlinked activities becomes skewed, then the city becomes dysfunctional. You have too many doctors and not enough food. Or too many bureaucrats and not enough people producing anything to pay for it all.

We have only to think of what happens in wartime to see how tyranny in any quarter creates hell for the rest.

No doubt many will maintain that they themselves provide the most important and most vital service to the life of the city. But that is human nature, personal pride. Why should one not take pride in one's contribution to the betterment of human kind? Be proud of what you do and contribute. Fine.

However, there are those who would, for whatever reasons: ideology, self-aggrandizement or plain greed, place one or other aspect of the city (theirs) above all others. And if those people somehow gain the upper hand, through political power, religious dogma, or the mis-use of wealth, they will distort the city to shape it in their own likeness, making it ugly, and making the lives of all its inhabitants less than they might otherwise be.

The Net-Hook Fallacy

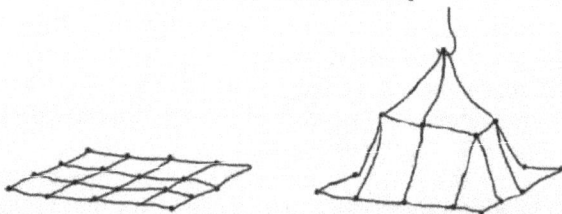

One aspect of a networked system receives more attention, funding, power, resources, or time than the rest and this distorts the whole, leaving the whole to operate less than optimally and possibly entirely dysfunctionally.
The fallacy is the mistaken belief that this distortion is needed in order to achieve good overall functionality, or to comply with dogma.

Figure 4: The Net-Hook Fallacy. When the emphasis is counter-productive. When an efficient and equitable system is sacrificed to greed, dogma, or sheer folly.

their students.

If we think of our interlinked city as a net or web made up of fine strands of twine, knotted together where they intersect, then it is as if a hook has caught on one single knot in the web and dragged that knot above all others, elevating those knots closest to it, but in effect turning a flat network into a hierarchy (Figure 4).

A hierarchy is easier to run—in fact the idea is often to turn the city into something that can be run, rather than leaving it with maximum autonomy, in which everyone might find their own place, leaving the city the freedom to self-adjust to be fair and efficient[88].

The Net-Hook Fallacy is the error of imposing a hierarchy on a network of essentially equal parts by elevating the role of one single part and making the rest subservient to it, believing this to be the right order of things (or, at least justifying the action by some specious appeal to e.g. the 'public good'[89]).

Hierarchies, while convenient for those who enjoy exercising power, and reaping the benefits of power, do not automatically best serve the needs of all those so governed. It might happen by accident, but I suggest that this is rare and difficult. Hierarchies do not automatically provide a panacea for all complex systems.

In another example, a similar error can be made in law-making.

Draconian laws might be imposed on the whole of society on the back of the justification that some single terrible evil *must be stopped*. To object simply that such a law is 'unbalanced', 'incommensurate', or 'disproportionate' is to present one's opposition along a single dimension. As if the new law impacts only one thing; inconveniences us all, but only in one minor aspect of our lives.

But these draconian laws have side effects, knock-on effects, and consequences both seen and unseen; their

---

88 Not unlike the cellular automata in This Robot Brain Gets Life, LoD 2023, where interactions are regulated but outcomes are not dictated.

89 Often, politicians will announce 'targets' and 'priorities' and, given that you cannot manage what you cannot measure, they introduce metrics which will no doubt confirm the success of their policies. Of course what happens is the city becomes a slave to the metric, and where metrics cannot be met, and the penalty for not meeting them is tangible—the metrics will be falsified. Some other way must be found (ask the man who saved schools).

implementation is linked to sufficiently many other aspects of society that they distort all of society. Those advocating such laws commit the Net-Hook Fallacy.

Remember: a neurotic becomes fixated on a single aspect of life at the expense of all else. That is no way to live. For any of us.

WHAT HAS THIS got to do with Art of any kind?
It has everything to do with the nature of the artist and the artistic endeavour.

If artists are skilled in their craft and communicate some shared human truth they must draw on all of their experience, not only to capture the truth with all its nuances, but to touch as many human souls as possible.

To use Art as a means to package advertising is crass, but to use it for propaganda to convey an unbending message (usually of oppression) is shameful. Such practitioners demean Art and turn it into mere design for the message.

Thus the Net-Hook fallacy reveals how a genuine aesthetic gets subverted.

An actor that successfully embraces the part he plays of a refugee from tyranny can be engaging and compelling and convey to the audience some of what that dreadful situation must be like. He can touch their souls.

But the actor who did not flee the same tyranny, and who now acts in infomercials about how wonderful grain production is in the state (or how we shall all be poor but happy—whatever the vile mantra of choice), has demeaned his art, abused his craft, and is a mere propagandist.

No single simple message can ever be an aesthetic truth. Even 'universal truths' are clichés and carry truth only to the degree that their vagueness allows. To promote one such is to commit the Net-Hook Fallacy, and for the Artist, is *inauthentic*.

ART HAS CONTENT; it is a communication.
But it is not a message; art that messages is propaganda, or advertising, or graphic design above all else. It is cognitive first and any aesthetic[90] quality comes a poor second.
Only sensations that are available directly in The Surface can be candidates for aesthetic experience.

---

90 Swiftly and justifiably condemned to become cliché.

Cognitive content is never felt experience. It may be appreciated, and the brain may assert Meaning[M] in relation to various cognitions during its cogitations, but an aesthetic response is only possible in directly experienced qualia.

Moreover, as soon as art[a] teaches, preaches, or proselytizes it no longer speaks from the soul[91]. Lecturing (hounding the audience with a cognitive message[92]) corrupts all aesthetic sensibilities and removes all possible subtlety and nuance that might otherwise have accumulated in a fully rendered view of the complex and difficult world in which struggle.

Such art[a] delivers nothing that cannot be obtained from newspaper headlines. Besides, all propaganda must be false[93] and yet will always be presented as truth.

Nothing could be more inauthentic.

Worse is too come.

For the artist, even their finest aesthetic production may be reduced to cliché because the work becomes widely recognised as worthy.

This is not to say that popular art somehow merely by being popular becomes a lesser thing. What happens is, the popularity of the work leads to its wide adoption for promotional purposes, and for merchandise. The work becomes a commonplace, a cliché.

We hardly glance at it before looking away. We hardly hear it before tuning into something else. We see the words on the page and skim over them, hardly engaged:

To be, or not to be—Yeah, yeah, yeah—Yada, yada, yada—Get a move on—We all know about you!

There is no aesthetic response; we have already dismissed it (i.e. cognitively) before the details or any nuances reach The Surface (that is, if the resolution of the

---

91 The present text is a philosophical piece and makes no claim to art.

92 Cognitive messages are not felt in The Surface; they have Meaning(M) in the same way as mathematics. Like so-called 'conceptual art' they do not generate a sensory aesthetic response.

93 Truth being a subtle, difficult, and nuanced thing; if it were not—if it were easy—why is it so hard to identify, or have AIs reproduce?

reproduction even allows us to see the brushstrokes or hear the emotional crackle in the voice).

The artist has expressed themselves so successfully that they end up failing to generate any aesthetic response at all.

It's pretty but is it art?

It's Art but you stopped seeing, hearing, or otherwise engaging with it.

AND THAT SPEAKS to the heart of the Net-Hook Fallacy.

Ultimately, Art[A] is simplicity borne of complexity, not of ignorance.

How can a single line in a Picasso portrait capture the essence of a unique human being? Yet it can. Each line draws [sic] on all aspects of the mental network of the artist's skill and felt experience. The line is not merely some part of some map of literal representation, or cognitive assessment, played out by hand.

The portrait is not some functional photographic reproduction[94], or cartoonish approximation[95]; the artist has engaged with the human being who is the sitter, and expressed their relationship.

Similarly the sound emitted by a perfect pitch machine cannot be Art[A] because the real, expressive voice has been removed and replaced by the sounds of a machine.

And when it comes to AI, AI has no felt connection to a feeling, seeing, hearing human being. AI has no Truth[T] at all, to tell.

Besides all of which, Artists, in the end, must think for themselves, never toe a party line. They must seek and sup on the broadest hinterland of the mind or else commit the Net-Hook Fallacy.

An artist, to be authentic, must arrive at an informed naivety; to connect as if seeing the world for the first time; to use cognition as no more that an aid to craft and skill; to connect to the world as they find it, to judge not, but to pass on the complexity and subtlety of human frailty to whomsoever stumbles across their work.

~

---

94 I have in mind a passport photograph. I would not deny artistic expression to a photographer per se.

95 As for photography, so for any aesthetic skill, of course.

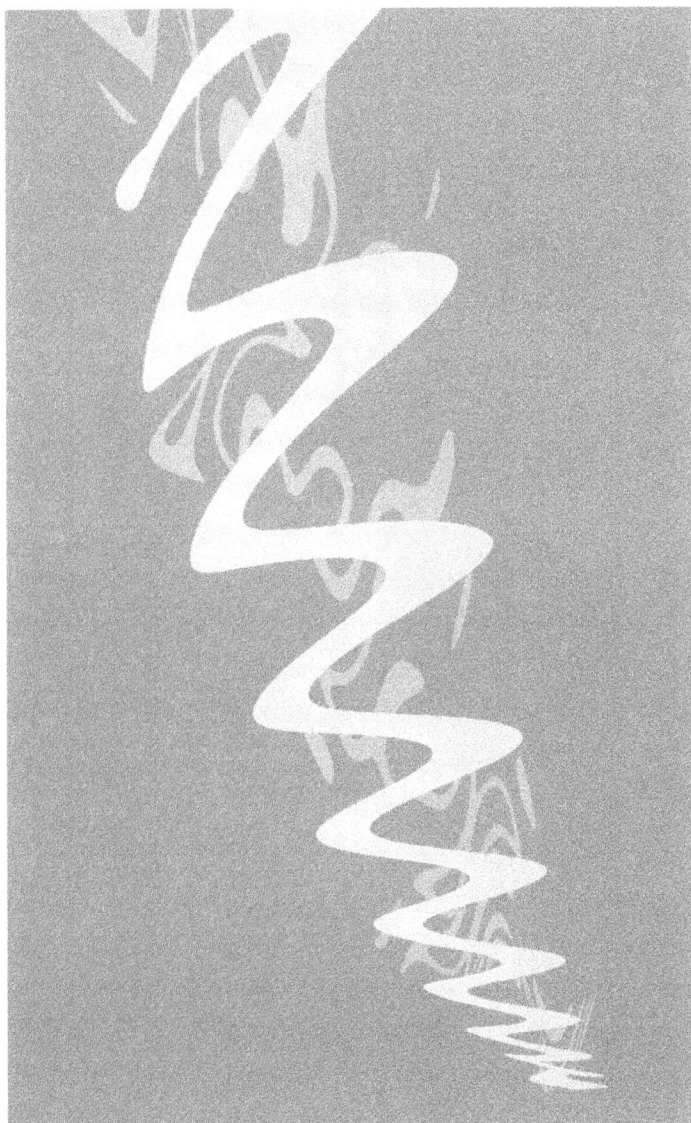

What Next?

If you'd like to read (or listen to) more from Jack Calverley, join his Patreon for free, for updates, as soon as new material becomes available:

https://patreon.com/JackCalverley